ALSO BY TONY KORNHEISER

The Baby Chase
Pumping Irony

BALD AS I WANNA BE

BALD AS I WANNA BE

TONY KORNHEISER

VILLARD

NEW YORK

Library of Congress Cataloging-in-Publication Data

Kornheiser, Tony.
Bald as I wanna be / Tony Kornheiser.
p.   cm.
ISBN 0-375-50037-5
I. Title.
PN4874.K67B35   1997
814'.54—dc21   97-19384

Random House website address: http://www.randomhouse.com/
Printed in the United States of America on acid-free paper
24689753
First Edition

For Jake and Anita;
Laz and Julie

Contents

Introduction / xi

It's a Jungle Out There / 1

This Is What I Come Home To / 77

Fear of Fogeyism / 121

He Said . . . She Said . . . / 167

Going Mobile / 187

Rich, Famous People Who Don't Know I Exist / 209

Capital Comment / 251

Acknowledgments / 269

Introduction

This is my second collection of columns, coming on the heels of the critically acclaimed *Pumping Irony*.

Well, perhaps critically acclaimed is an overstatement.

I did fabulously well in the overseas press. The reviewer in *Hola Argentina* called me "*un pedazo de pescado asqueroso*," which I'm fairly certain means I'm a humor god in Buenos Aires.*

The bad news is that I was reviewed in only one place in English.

The good news is that it was in *The New York Times*.

The New York Times!

Not every book gets reviewed in *The New York Times*, which is so august it only has room to comment on the very, very best books—and, of course, every word ever written about important pre-Raphaelite sculptors. So I was very proud that the *Times* would review me. And I was very hopeful that it would be a glowing review, because I had been a reporter at the *Times*, and I had made friends among those few people in the Sunday book section who were actually still alive when they worked there reviewing books. (My writing at the *Times* had been considered quite avant-garde, because I wasn't slavishly observant of the *Times* stylebook. For example, I once violated official *Times*

---

* Actually, I'm wrong—it's a disgustingly smelly piece of fish.

style by referring to "a small cylindrical object designated to surround and transport products or goods" as "a box.")

To review my book the *Times* assigned a woman of such importance that she had three names: Ruth Bayard Smith.

Here are the very words she wrote about my collected columns:

> They're sophomoric: what's special about the first spring day when the ice cream man shows up? It "coincides with the first day women resume wearing halter tops." They're offensive: on an objection by math teachers that the Barbie doll was programmed to say that math is tough, he writes, "Girls are—how shall I put this sensitively—stupid in math." The best piece in the book is a candid and humorous account of a course Mr. Kornheiser took to combat his fear of flying. But not much else in *Pumping Irony* is as sincere or rings as true, unless some readers see honesty in his account of cleaning his ears with a Q-tip.

(That Q-tip thing was one of my best, by the way. You should have seen the gunk that came out of my ears. It came out in one big, furry ball that was about the size of one of those arrowhead erasers. I feared it was alive. I didn't know whether to step on it or put it on a leash.)

At first I was hurt by this unrelenting, vicious, personal attack by a babe with three names who, for all I know, looks like a sow in a halter top. But then I was able to pull out some key words that I thought would help sales:

"Special! Best! Humorous! Sincere! True! Ears!"—*The New York Times.*

Some writers might be devastated by such a review, and might never write again. (Not me. I have no shame whatsoever.) But the more I thought about it, the more I realized "sophomoric" and "offensive" were pretty much what I was aiming for. So I felt pretty good about it. I felt like those high school toughs in the opening scene of the film *Broadcast News* who beat up the valedictorian on graduation day. And then the valedictorian picks himself up and wipes the blood off his nose and yells scathingly at his tormentors, "Just remember this. You can beat me up now, but years from now, when I'm a famous reporter and I come back to this poor, pathetic hovel in triumph, you'll all still be working at the meat plant, making nineteen thousand dollars a year." And the young toughs look at each other and say, "Nineteen thousand, huh? Not bad."

Sophomoric, huh? Not bad. At least I got through freshman year.

Anyway, it is with some trepidation that I release this book. I wanted to write something Ruth Bayard Smith would like, something profound, something serious, something with gravitas. But I couldn't come up with enough columns on the deconstruction of the American socioeconomic infrastructure to make a whole book. So I threw in some of the usual crap.

Ruthie, this one's for you.

IT'S A
JUNGLE
OUT THERE

Coffee, Tea, Or . . . ?

It's not easy being a famous, beloved columnist. The world is a carnival of events and activities, and deciding which to write about can be an ordeal. Take this week, for example. I had two logical choices:

1. "Worldwide Tensions Simmer as UN Celebrates Fiftieth Anniversary." While ethnic violence still rages in Bosnia, while a shaky peace is still threatened by flare-ups in the Middle East, while war-crimes tribunals convene in Rwanda and human-rights violations continue in China, leaders from 137 nations gathered in New York to see if the United Nations retains viability as a structure for global peace and understanding as it enters an uncertain middle age.

2. "Airline Passenger Poops on Food-Service Cart."

You can stop calling now, I think we've got a winner.

First-class passenger Gerard Finneran, fifty-eight, president of an investment banking company, allegedly got so drunk and abusive on a recent flight from Buenos Aires to New York, and so steamed that he would not be served additional drinks, that he climbed atop the service cart like an orangutan, dropped his pants, and

(Note to copy desk: Please insert some classy euphemism here, so we don't lose any additional readers.)

. . . delivered a cruller.

Talk about being three sheets to the wind: Finneran then allegedly used the first-class linen napkins to, um, tidy up afterward. How's that for a coup de gross? Lucky he wasn't in coach, with those paper napkins the texture of acoustic tile.

Think back to your school days, about the most embarrassing thing you ever did while drunk. In my case it was puking on my girlfriend's parents' chiffonier. Compared with what this guy allegedly did, puking on a chiffonier is like being ordained an archbishop.

Hoo boy, I'll bet the other passengers were ticked. Out of concern for possible contamination, the captain cut off all food and beverage service—with four hours left in the flight. Wow. You've got to go four more hours with the Count of Caca, and you can't get so much as a shot of Scotch and a bagel with a schmear? So to speak.

(Note to copy desk: Whaddaya think? Is ANYONE still reading this?)

(Possibly some guys in a grunge band, Tony.)

(Note to copy desk: Let me take care of that right now.)
How drunk was this guy?
STINKING drunk. Hahahahaha.
(Okay, good work, Tony. We're down to zero now. Um, do WE have to keep reading?)

Actually, I don't care how drunk he was. How could someone do something like this? All I can think of is that he hated the bathrooms in planes as much as I do. I'm terrified to be in an airplane bathroom. It's tiny, and it's cramped, and it bounces and rattles like a box of elbow macaroni on a Tilt-A-Whirl. I feel as if it's been Super-Glued onto the plane. And my fear—and the fear of any sane person—is that it will detach from the plane. My idea of a nightmare is plummeting thirty thousand feet to my death over Kansas with my pants around my ankles while seated on an aluminum pooper the size of a flowerpot.

Anyway, this guy is the president of an investment banking firm! (He's fifty-eight. He works on Wall Street. I didn't think guys like that even *mooned* anybody.) Can you imagine any worse news for a company than for its president to do this? Let me put it this way: They're even laughing at this around the water cooler at Tylenol!

What toast did Finneran offer before his last drink? Bottoms up?

I'm wondering how it went when the board of directors of his company asked President Finneran exactly what happened on that plane.

I imagine he had a series of explanation strategies prepared.

Strategy No. 1: "I have never even flown on an airplane. At the time of the alleged incident I was practicing sand shots in my backyard."

No. 2: (Oh, wow. No. 2, get it?)

No. 3: "I have no recall of doing anything like this at this particular time. I suppose it's possible, in a theoretical sense, that I could have done this. But it doesn't sound like something I would have done."

(I read a story about this incident, and a friend of Finneran was quoted saying, "It seems so out of character for him." Who the hell *doesn't* it seem out of character for?)

I'm thinking ahead a few years, when the, uh, aroma of this incident fades and Finneran is back in the investment game—maybe flying to Zurich for a meeting. Maybe the airlines will have put his picture up in every galley with a note: DO NOT SERVE THIS MAN A DRINK. AND FOR HEAVEN'S SAKE DO NOT LET HIM NEAR THE LINENS.

Some of us were talking about what would possibly be worse than being stuck in a plane with this guy for four hours, and somebody suggested being stuck in an elevator. Someone else, a smarter person, said a bathysphere.

The one circumstance we could agree would be worse than being on this plane with Finneran would be if we were in a space capsule with him, two days into a six-day mission. Because of the zero-gravity thing.

I'm Tony. Buy Me.

This space available:

Yes, I am selling out.

If Mario Cuomo and Ann Richards can sell corn chips, and if Michael Jordan can lend his name to a McDonald's *bacon cheeseburger*—I mean, give *me* a break today!

It's just a matter of time before we have the Merrill Lynch State of the Union address. Any day now I expect Al

D'Amato to endorse Odor-Eaters, and the copy will say, "As a guy who puts my foot in my mouth . . ."

Everybody's selling out.

And now so am I. You can buy space in this column.

Let me take the trouble of anticipating your questions:

Q. Why should I buy space in your column, Tony?

A. Because I am a very influential journalist in the most important media outlet in the most important city in the United States. In all humility, I'm No. 1 in the capital of the Free World! So getting me on your side is crucial to the success of your corporate venture.

Q. Why you, though, and not some other big-shot columnist, like George F. Will?

A. Because I have the common touch; I use words that can be understood without placing a person-to-person call to William F. Buckley. And because I'll endorse *anything*! I'd endorse an impotency clinic and claim I'm a satisfied customer. I'd endorse Kaopectate one week and toilet paper the next. I have no shame. But back to me and Will. Let's say your firm wants a trusted, important journalist to say something nice about E-Z Cheez. I've actually tasted the product. I've sprayed it on crackers, and I've sprayed it on my index finger and licked it clean. Does George F. Will strike you as the kind of man who sprays cheese?

Q. What do you charge for your services?

A. Good question! I have three advertising packages available: The first, silver, costs $5,000. This makes you "a friend of Tony." The next, gold, costs $10,000. It makes you "a good friend of Tony." The top-of-the-line package, platinum, costs $20,000. It makes you "Tony's current love interest."

And here's what you get!

Let's use Coca-Cola as an example.

For $5,000 I will drop in a line like, "Coke. I drink it all the time. My, it's good." Imagine the impact that will have in the middle of a column about, say, all the ways Phil Gramm reminds me of Mr. Potato Head. I can hear the cans opening now.

For $10,000 I will drop in an even stronger line like, "Drinking Coke has dramatically increased the size of my genitals." People identify with me. If it works for me, it'll work for them.

For $20,000 I will give you my most dedicated service. I'll assassinate your rival with a line like, *I've heard if you drink Pepsi, you'll go blind.* I will italicize it and put it on the front page of the column, "before the jump," as we say in the trade.

(I am also syndicated in many major markets. I can tailor your message to fit a specific area. For instance, I am syndicated in the *Seattle Times.* Seattle is big on chichi coffee. You might want to "direct-buy" Seattle. In the midst of a sports column about an outfielder who'd been brought up to the majors for a cup of coffee, I could artfully throw in that it was "Starbucks coffee. I drink it. You should too.")

This is a lot cheaper than taking out a standard ad in

this newspaper, which would cost you $25,000 or so. Nobody actually reads those ads. Everybody reads me. You got this far, didn't you?

Q. How do we pay you, Tony?

A. Very easy. You just make a check out to my housekeeper, and she cashes it and gives it to my brother.

Let me again repeat the way this works. This time we'll use a restaurant as an example. Your fine gourmet establishment is called "Ernie's L'Dew Drop Inn." Now, let's say the column I'm writing is about what a dish Benazir Bhutto is, and I've just gotten to the part where I describe what Ms. Bhutto is eating during the interview.

For $5,000 I'll write, "Benazir Bhutto picked daintily at her pâté de campagne . . . which is nice if you're from Pakistan, I guess. Personally, I prefer the crispy chicken drenched in nacho cheese at Ernie's L'Dew Drop Inn, $4.95 all you can eat weekdays until 4. Man, that's good."

For $10,000 I'll write, "Benazir Bhutto picked daintily at her pâté de campagne . . . then she looked deeply into my eyes and said, 'I've never met a man as handsome and selfassured and virile as you. I think I love you. Take me here, now, on the table. But first, tell me your secret for mastery over women.' And I said, 'I eat all my meals at Ernie's L'Dew Drop Inn, where the food's great and the service is greater. Children's menu available.' "

For $20,000 I'll write, "Benazir Bhutto picked daintily at her pâté de campagne . . . and she began looking quite sallow; the color drained from her cheeks. I knew she couldn't have gotten bad food from Ernie's L'Dew Drop

Inn, where the elite meet to eat. 'Where's this food from?' I asked her. 'Al's,' she said, 'it's across the street from Ernie's.' *'Oh, no. Not Al's,'* I said, placing my hand on the back of Benazir's swanlike neck as she spewed all over the table. *'Everybody knows they serve roadkill at Al's.'*"

Hey, I'm here for you.

All you gotta do is call.

A Fragrant Foul

I have the new Michael Jordan Cologne in my office. I don't actually have a bottle. I have a sample card that I picked up at Foot Locker—which, I admit, is not generally my first choice for shopping for a personal fragrance. I sniffed the card, found the odor rather perky, left it on my desk, and thought nothing more about it until my friend Nancy walked in the office and asked me if I'd had the carpet sprayed for scarab-beetle infestation.

"It's like five guys have been in here using industrial-strength Right Guard and shellac," she said.

Surely by now you've seen the TV ads for this stuff. The screen starts out a fiery tomato red. Then black bubbles up, haphazardly at first, like in a lava lamp, until finally it congeals in the form of Jordan's head—or a fire hydrant. Then you see the words: "Michael Jordan Cologne."

You know, if I were looking for Michael Jordan's next product—understanding that he already sells everything, including *underpants!*—a fragrance would be the last thing I'd think of. Michael Jordan is in the business of sweating. Putting him together with cologne is like having Christie Brinkley sell feminine mustache bleach, or Carl Sagan endorsing the Psychic Hot Line. My friend Gino said that if you gave the average person a sheet of paper and instructions to list what he thinks of when he thinks of Michael Jordan, "smells good" would end up No. 97, right after "rabbinical student."

But judging from recent news that Air Jordan sneakers are going for as much as two thousand dollars a pair in Japan, it seems clear that people will buy anything Michael Jordan is selling. So, to protect the rights of American citizens, the world-renowned Kornheiser Consumer Advocacy Group (registered in Indonesia on the advice of the DNC) conducted an impartial scientific investigation to ascertain the desirability of the product.

I put the sample in an old cardboard box. Then Nancy and I proceeded into the newsroom, asking people to close their eyes, stick their heads in the box, and tell us what they smelled.

We started in the sports department. What better place?

"Dead leaves in my gutters from the winter that I'm

cleaning in the spring, with my gloves on because they're so gloppy," announced my friend Tracee, who put the *o* in olfactory.

"My ninth-grade physical-science teacher, Mr. Eissens," Bonnie said.

A couple of men poked their noses in, then withdrew, saying it smelled like perfume, sweet and fruity.

"I like it," said Allison. "It's kind of musky and outdoorsy."

"I said it was outdoorsy," Tracee piped up. "It smells like my toolshed, where I found the dead squirrel—that's outdoorsy."

We took our fumes to the art department, hoping for something more sensitive.

"Smells good," somebody said.

"No, it doesn't. It smells like some guy's armpits," somebody else said.

"It's Michael Jordan Cologne," I informed them, and one of these creative souls suggested maybe it was deliberately, uh, pungent—for guys who just finished playing basketball and don't have time to shower, to keep in the glove compartment for a quick dousing on the way to pick up a date.

"Ugh," Carol said indignantly. "Let me tell you something. There's nothing worse than funk covered up by sweet cologne. Guys who do that better get hosed down heavy."

Next we tried the Style section. After all, the publicity kit that accompanied the cologne said, "Michael Jordan is the essence of style."

An editor I shan't name (you'll see why) said it "smells like *Esquire* magazine."

Perfect! These days popular glossy magazines—*Esquire, GQ, Vanity Fair*—are chock full of peel-and-sniff cologne ads. Personally, I never buy cologne anymore. I simply subscribe to magazines. "As soon as I get the magazine," I said, "I rub it all over my face."

He looked at me quizzically. "Your face?" he said. "Yes, that's a thought."

Hmmmm.

Rita said it had a "poofy" smell—then implored me to go away because the smell was making her nauseated.

Joel sniffed twice. "It's a urinal cake, right?"

(Nancy, who has not liberated a men's room since the 1960s, did not know that urinal cakes exist. I got angry at Joel for bringing it up. "It's the one thing men have left that women don't know about," I told him. "Now they'll want them, too. I hope you're happy.")

Robin the Fashion Queen already knew about the cologne. She had received a publicity kit, which actually contains these words: "We created a scent that allows the wearer to feel a little closer to what Michael's Jordan's life is like each and every day."

You mean we get to smell Dennis Rodman, too?

In addition to its dopey prose ("We have built a fragrance note by note, using innovative headspace technology"), the publicity kit has little samples of the five fragrance "accords" used in the cologne. These are called "rare air," "cool," "pebble beach," "home run," and "sensual."

No joke.

We smelled each of those accords separately. "Rare air" smells like nothing at all. It was the emperor's new scent. "Cool" was clearly a shot of gin. "Home run" smelled like sweat. "Pebble beach" smelled like old white guys in plaid pants, and I couldn't place "sensual"; it was somewhere between a wet dog and David Falk, Jordan's agent.

Sadly, Robin the Fashion Queen is no fan of Michael Jordan Cologne. She believes it smells like "a really sleazy 1980s disco—like the guy coming out of the bathroom."

You mean a personal foul?

The 80-Proof Workout

Nothing but bad news: War in Bosnia. Ferry capsizes off Finland. Chaos in Haiti. Baseball strike. Hockey strike . . .

It makes you wanna have a drink.

Go ahead. Matter of fact, have two.

I've just poured myself a tumbler of Scotch the size of Costa Rica. Later on, I'll have another. And when I'm done, I'll be healthy as a horse. I won't finish typing this column, of course—I won't be able to see the keys—but I'll feel great!

At least that's what a study reported in the *Journal of the American Medical Association* says. The study tested 631 male doctors and found that the ones who had two or more drinks every day were the least likely to suffer heart attacks—which stands to reason, because how much stress can you feel when you've passed out on a gurney? At least now we know why doctors have such terrible handwriting.

(Should we be concerned that the study was conducted on doctors? I don't necessarily want the medical group of Dr. Jim Beam and Dr. Johnnie Walker removing my appendix. I mean, would you be confident if the last words you heard before the anesthesia kicked in were: "Scalpel. Sutures. Seagram's!" Personally, I'd have preferred if they tested all 631 daytime talk-show hosts to find out how many drinks it'd take to make them stop doing O.J. shows.)

But docs aside, this is great news, isn't it?

It means a comeback for the three-martini lunch. Which is a win-win situation. Not only will the martinis prevent heart attacks, but olives are a source of the good cholesterol!

We can drink our way to good health. Now I know there's a God.

How about pie? Oh, please tell me pie is good too.

(You know who really must be delirious about this? Dean Martin. Because if two drinks a day keep you from getting a heart attack, that guy must be immortal by now; the only way Dino can go is if somebody strikes a match near him. *[Editor's Note: For those of you who are confused by reference to Dean Martin, think of him as the Sinbad of his day.]*)

Here's what we know now that we didn't know a few years ago (but hoped):

1. Liquor is good.

2. Margarine is bad.

3. Oat bran tastes like shirt cardboard, and is almost as good for you.

4. There's *good* cholesterol.

5. Bruce Willis has no career.

Given the way the tides are shifting, is it too much to hope that soon muscle tone won't be considered attractive and bald spots will? Because I could be a god.

How about suntans? Could the dermatologists be wrong about the sun? Then I could go to the beach without wrapping my body in so much gauze that I look like Katharine Hepburn on the way to a Hindu funeral.

I am so happy with this study. Not only is it good news for the average Joe who likes to get so schnockered on Saturday night that he wakes up Sunday morning with his head in the litter box, but it's also bad news for the self-righteous twits who have lorded their "healthy lifestyle" over us. You know who I mean: those preachy creeps who don't smoke or drink and threaten to call up that loony bald babe Susan Powter if they catch you using real sugar in your coffee; the yuppie losers at the bar swilling down that repulsive nonalcoholic beer that tastes like the Green Bay Packers ran a garden hose over their feet and put it in a bottle.

Now there's one less patch on the moral high ground for them to stand on. Hopefully, this will start the revolution in the exercise field: fewer knee bends, more elbow bends. I'm reminded of the day fitness guru Jim Fixx died. Not that I wished him ill, but let's face it—he was setting a bad example. He didn't drink or smoke, he ate those green things—what are they called, vegetables? He flossed between meals, and he ran from Pittsburgh to Denver every afternoon. A guy like that makes you feel so inadequate. So when he dropped dead in the middle of a jog . . . well, like most of you I allowed myself a moment of silence—and then opened another bag of potato chips.

Good health is killing us! Well, it's killing our taste buds anyway. The White House chef was fired because he wouldn't cook low-fat meals. He was a French chef, for heaven's sake, not Kate Moss. You can't drink real soda anymore, it's got to be flavored with NutraSweet, and you know there'll be a study within five years that discovers NutraSweet will kill you; it's probably made from goat hoofs. You can't cook eggs with butter—it'll clog your arteries and kill you halfway through your omelet—so you end up coating the pan with that spray starch. I mean, why not simply eat your shirt? Anyway, you can't eat real eggs— the yolks will kill you. I imagine this huge processing plant where the eggs are separated, and somebody doing a Rodney Dangerfield impersonation, tugging at his collar and saying, "I tell ya, things are rough all over, yeah, rough; I don't get no respect; whaddaya want from me, these are the yolks!" Yeah, it's all going to hell for chickens. Eating their eggs is bad for us, eating their skin is bad for us. Though as bad as the chicken is for us, I've been to chicken coops, and I've got to believe we're worse for the chicken. Didya hear about the guy who went to the psychiatrist and said, "My brother thinks he's a chicken," and the psychiatrist said, "Well, why don't you bring him to see me?" And the man said: "We need the eggs." And then there was the time . . .

(Editor's Note: At press time, Mr. Kornheiser was sleeping off the effects of his medical research. His column will resume next week.)

Influenza and Out the Door

You'll please excuse me if I interrupt this column from time to time to dash to the bathroom. I have the flu.

There are apparently two kinds of flu. One starts in your throat with an annoying dryness and a gagging sensation and eventually spreads to your head, your chest, your back, and your legs—nothing you need, unless you plan to live through the week—and produces nausea, aches, tiredness, sneezing, a voice like Baba Wawa, and an overwhelming desire to leap off the nineteenth-floor parapet of the Hyatt Regency and land flush on that idiot woman playing the harp in the lobby at seven in the morning. This flu lasts five days, or until the chicken fat begins to seep through your pores and you hear yourself say *"bggawwk, bggawwk"* when your kids ask if you'd like some more soup.

The other flu starts in your stomach and hunkers down there like a tribe of squatters. It produces simultaneous diarrhea and vomiting, the old D&V, which leaves you confused as to which way to turn—and wondering where God got His zany sense of humor. You dare not eat or drink a thing. To what end? Literally. How can you eat? Your teeth feel like rutabagas, and your tongue looks like the thing that burst out of the guy's solar plexus in *Alien.* The doctor says you should drink to avoid dehydration. Oh, dehydration is bad? This is a romp in the park, but *dehydration* is what will kill me? Good, give me dehydration. This flu lasts twenty-four hours—the longest twenty-four hours since PBS ran *A Day in the Life of Elliot Richardson*—nearly all of which you spend in close proximity to a tile floor asking how you could have been so stupid as to cut class the day they went over *this* in biology.

Lucky me. I have both.

(Excuse me. Be right back.)

(Thanks.)

I've spent the last eight hours taking measurements around my house. I want to know exactly how far it is to the bathrooms from anywhere. I want to know if I can make it, or should I just order new carpet now?

"Flu is a good topic to write about," my friend Norman said. "It's really going around now. I just talked to Vinnie—he was hacking up something green."

I knew I was going to get the flu. It was just a matter of time. Five days ago my son had it. He threw up four times. Two days ago my daughter had it. She threw up eight times. I knew when my turn rolled around I was looking at double figures. Yesterday morning I got the first telltale signs, the fogginess in the forehead and the perpetual squint. By noon, my skin felt like I'd fallen asleep on a radiator. I spent the afternoon thinking what a waste of money it was sending 400,000 troops to Iraq when we could just Express Mail my flu to Saddam.

(Oops. Be back in a second.)

Children are unbothered by the flu. They get it, no big deal. The older you get, though, the greater the dread. Let's suppose we could choose which kind of flu to have— the five-day ache-all-over malaise or the twenty-four-hour fire-hose blast. A college student will invariably select the shorter, more intense flu. What's throwing up to them? Nothing. They do it all the time. It's like a lab science. A quick *rrrrralph*, and they're back at the keg. Now, a mature forty-year-old adult might be tempted to walk the same route, and this would be a terrible blunder, because you forget how *unbelievably awful and disgusting* throwing up is if you haven't done it in fifteen or twenty years. I wouldn't wish it on a dog. I take that back. I would wish it on a dog. Just not a dog in my house.

Amazingly, some people think the flu is fun—my smart friend Martha, who hardly ever gets sick, for example. She actually enjoys it. "My favorite part," she said—*her favorite part!*—"is when your hair hurts so you can't brush it, and you can walk around with it sticking straight up. It really adds to the ambiance. I learned this from my mother, the

2 4

opera singer. She'd get a cold, and it was Mimi's death scene from *La Boheme.*"

At least the flu these days isn't what it was a hundred years ago. Then it was an epidemic. Deaths from the flu pandemic of 1918–1919 numbered in the millions! America's best-loved feature writer, Mr. Henry, points out, "That was when men were men and flu was flu." That was the golden age of flu. Now it's all these designer flus:

Swine flu, horrible to contemplate. You find you have an unquenchable urge to block for Mark Rypien. (I was suspicious of the logic of the swine-flu shot. Why let them inject you with a small dose of the flu to build an immunity? Would you let a doctor pump you with a .22 so you'd be immune later if you got whacked with a .357 Magnum? I think not.)

Type-A flu, which affects those with neurotic, overachieving personalities. John Sununu routinely gets this flu.

(The Rockin' Pneumonia and the) Boogie-Woogie flu.

Chimney flu, particularly prevalent Christmas Eve, when fat fathers stupidly get stuck in the brickwork pretending to be Santa Claus.

One Flu Over the Cuckoo's Nest, treatable by lobotomy.

Doug Flutie, a particularly short, scrambling flu.

Mr. Henry believes flu has been devalued, like the letter *X* in the name of a car to designate a souped-up model. It used to be only daredevil drivers like Stirling Moss got behind the wheel of an *X* car. Now everything—except my

Chevette, of course—has an *X* in it. (My Chevette is a turbo.)

"Nobody gets a cold anymore," Mr. Henry says. "A cold is as rare as Creutzfeldt-Jakob syndrome," which, as Mr. Henry well knows, is a degenerative neurological disease isolated in the South Pacific islands that one might acquire by eating other people's brains. (No thanks, I'll stick with the fried shrimp.) "Everything is the flu. You can hardly call your boss and say, 'I won't be in today. I have *a cold.*' You have to have the flu. Nobody gets a cold. Nobody gets the trots. Nobody gets a headache. It's automatically the flu."

Not tonight, dear, I have the flu.

Or, as we might say in a few years, when the flu goes the way of the common cold, "Not tonight, dear, I have Creutzfeldt-Jakob syndrome."

Oh! Can you take it the rest of the way without me?

Gotta run.

Ad Infinitum

A few years ago a brand-new car, Infiniti, was introduced through an artsy advertising campaign that consisted of pictures of rocks, forests, water, and birds. There was no car, which I suspect confused people, and may account for the fact that Infiniti sold only twelve cars nationwide in the next eighteen months—although the Sierra Club got 43 million new members.

Now Infiniti uses an advertising campaign that consists entirely of a man and a car. You know what they're selling: It is an automobile—and if you shut the window, you can drown out the cackling from those damn birds.

Skimming over a chichi magazine recently, I flipped through *nine straight pages* labeled "Polo Sport Ralph Lauren," which I guess is supposed to be a line of clothing. But the majority of the ads were bewildering, since I didn't know whether Ralph was selling clothes or vacation time shares. In one ad, two pages wide, there were ten sailboats in a race—but no visible sailors. The same pages included a picture of an American flag. (Is he selling flags now? Where does he put the logo?) Another page was devoted totally to a nail-polish-red sports car— no clothing there. There was a page with a man climbing the icy face of a mountain, but he was so small he looked like a wad of gum stuck in a defrosting freezer. Another full-page ad featured a beautiful, mysterious woman in a skintight ski suit who seemed to be saying to me, "I wouldn't date you if you were the last thing walking upright on Earth."

Mercedes-Benz is less subtle about what it's selling: an irredeemably overpriced car with grotesque baby windshield wipers on the headlights. And to give you a convenient excuse for spending an unforgivable sum of money, they run TV ads showing crash dummies bouncing off a brick wall in what looks like Eva Braun's old bunker, and dress up some former buzz-bomb scientist in a lab coat to say, "Yes, ve have ze patent. But ve vouldn't dream of enforsing it. Zafety is too important." This allows you to tell friends you bought a Mercedes because it's so humanitarian—not because you want to stick it up your neighbor's kazoo.

But Mercedes may have blundered this time by announcing recently that it will build a plant in Alabama. Think about this: You're ready to pop for $85,000 on a car. You look in the glove compartment and see a sign that says: THIS MERCEDES-BENZ WAS HANDCRAFTED BY VERNON "FISH HEAD" CLAMPETT, TUSCALOOSA. THAT'LL BE 85 BIG ONES. I don't think so. (Maybe they'll sell in Alabama. But what about those numerical-combination door locks? This is calculus in Alabama. The whole state could be locked out of their 500SEL's with those ROOOLLL-TIDE vanity plates.)

When someone mentions "Mercedes," I just don't expect "Alabama." It doesn't feel right, like that Biosphere 2 in Arizona. When the people finally came out this week after two years, I yelled to my kids, "The Biosphere's landed!" They reminded me it never actually went up, it merely lay in the Arizona sun like a retiree.

What a phony-baloney the Biosphere is. It isn't science. It's another roadside attraction. You could buy tickets to walk around and peer in. It was a carnival ride masquerading as a petri dish.

Two years ago, eight morons climbed into this big fishbowl claiming it was self-sufficient. Then we find out that the air went bad, so they had to pump more in to keep everybody from croaking, and that they had stored food waiting for them, and later on someone smuggled in makeup. Makeup! (I have seen the future, and it requires lip gloss.)

About the only scientific benefit of the Biosphere is as a diet center. Everyone inside lost weight, an average of 14 percent. So I eagerly await the first Bio-Spa-Lady franchise.

The Biosphere wasn't what it seemed to be, and neither,

apparently, is the Rockefeller Foundation. Once, the mere mention of Rockefeller brought on paranoid visions of the Trilateral Commission's plot to take over the world. Now, the foundation gives four thousand dollars to some artists to paint cows.

That's right, paint cows.

I gather it's some sort of bizarre feminist pageant in Wyoming. A herd of seventy cows was to be outfitted with signs carrying verses about women's plight from frontier days—sort of a mooing version of weeknights at Betty Friedan's house.

As if this wasn't loopy enough, three artists intended to paint some of the cows—*the pregnant ones*—to symbolically link motherhood, female self-sacrifice, and, uh, pineapple cottage cheese?

"Cows are great, and so are women," said artist Sue Thornton. Yeah, the Chicago Bulls are great too, but you don't see me slapping a coat of Sherwin-Williams Penobscot blue on Michael Jordan.

Before the culture goes completely to hell, though, I am pleased to report a small victory: Miller Brewing Co. has mercifully decided to can its experiment with clear beer. Miller Clear now outski as brewski—an acknowledgment that true beer drinkers know beer should be exactly the same color as it enters and exits the body.

It's a terrible trend to take old standbys and bleach them clear, so they appear to be hygienically pure and healthy. What, it's so healthy that if you drink two six-packs you won't fall on your face in the middle of M

Street like any other slob? You think it's the *color* that gets you drunk?

There are far too many clear products on the market already. Clear Pepsi, clear deodorant, clear gasoline. What ever happened to the old days, when all anybody wanted was clear skin?

The Green Grass Grew All Around

I definitely have to mow my lawn today. I can't put it off any longer. The moment of truth came Thursday when I dispatched my nine-year-old into the backyard to retrieve a Wiffle ball and she disappeared up to her neck.

The last few days I've stood at my window and literally watched my grass grow. (It's not as boring as you think; I mean, if you like C-SPAN, you'll love this.) The grass was growing so fast and in such thick clumps, I was tempted to toss my Rogaine in the garbage and bury my head in the soil, in hopes that my hair might regenerate naturally.

Even if my lawn didn't need mowing today, I'd have to do it anyway because of Fred, the obsessive-compulsive who lives up the block. Like the robin that signals the start of spring, Ol' Fred firing up that Black & Decker officially proclaims the opening of Lawn Season. He was out there yesterday morning at eight, in his blue walking shorts and black socks, his legs as pale as chalk, clipping and bagging and mulching and edging like the Lawn Doctor from Hell. Fred's lawn is so neat, so perfectly manicured . . . it makes you want to soak it in gasoline and light it up like Kuwait.

Once Fred cuts his lawn, everybody else has to cut his lawn or face the shame factor. Because when Fred is done, he and his noisy wife, Janice, take a self-satisfied stroll around the block and as they pass your house—with your lawn sprouting up like Don King's hair—they'll shake their heads and mutter, "What a shame the Jacksons moved away."

So everyone cuts and mulches and clips, and the noise from the power mowers on a Sunday morning sounds like an invasion of killer bees. And you see the men out there in their ratty sleeveless undershirts, and the women in their Orvis-catalog gardening gloves and surgical masks (like they've scrubbed up in a MASH unit). You smell so much gas in the air, you might as well be living in Fairfax, out by that tank farm. And then it escalates, of course, when some yuppie who's just moved in hires a landscaper for his stupid little postage-stamp plot, and suddenly it's not good enough to grow regular grass. Now you have to get zoysia or fescue or pampas grass, and modulate the pH factor and the soil temperature. Until it finally dawns on you: You don't have a lawn anymore, what you have is eighty square feet of tropical fish.

God, I hate lawn care.

Heaven help you if your lawn mower breaks down. You're dead meat. You might as well file for Chapter 11. Because now the only kind of mower they're showing is a John Deere riding mower for $72,000. I like short grass as much as the next guy, but I'll be damned if I'm going to take out a mortgage on a lawn mower.

My backyard is the size of a large cake box. What's the point of my buying a riding mower? I couldn't even make a U-turn in my yard without running over the swing set. Ultimately, I'll do what so many middle-aged men do: stand on the curb and wait for the flatbed truck loaded with power mowers and gypsy freelance cutters to cruise by, and hail it like a cab. The guy who drives the truck was a heart surgeon in Guatemala until he realized the big money here was in cutting grass.

Man About Town Chip Muldoon used to rent a house near me. He didn't mow his lawn for months at a time, which infuriated his neighbors. It was so overgrown with chickweed and dandelions it looked like the putting green at the Bates Motel. One afternoon he was visited by two muscular men with the new issue of *Better Homes & Gardens* rolled up in their back pockets: Lawn Vigilantes who *suggested* he might want to bring his yard up to community standards. Chip told them to shove off. The next morning, he awoke with the head of a Poulan Weed Eater on his pillow. That day Chip was out on the corner hailing the Guatemalan heart surgeon.

It's a point of pride with me that I cut my own lawn.

Well, it's a point of pride that I cut my back lawn. I no longer have a front lawn. After years of flushing money down the toilet by falling for the chemical company's promise of a thicker, greener lawn—and invariably getting the same old brown patch of dirt by June (I just wanted something green; I'd have settled for frozen spinach)—I ripped out the front lawn completely and brought in a landscape architect.

His name was Pietro. He told me to think of my front yard as "an ecological canvas," and it was his task to "balance the horticultural harmonies." He handed me his card. It listed all the great universities of Europe where he'd studied. I said, "Pietro, I'm just looking for a few green plants, not someone who's giving the keynote address at the Rio Earth Summit."

Not to worry, he'd turn my front yard into "an agronomic tapestry." Then he said something in European that roughly translates into, "Make sure it's a cashier's check."

The good news is, I don't have to mow my front lawn anymore. Pietro made it into a permanent exhibit at the World's Fair. I have a Scottish heather perennial border, a profusion of imported African wildflowers, variegated pachysandra from Crete, a Malaysian teak bench, Peruvian stone carvings, and enough pampas grass to cover the Cisco Kid. The bad news is, every spring I have to replace and reconfigure and remulch. And I get socked for $1,850—about nine times what the Guatemalan heart surgeon would charge to cut my lawn and give me an angioplasty.

I'm thinking of going back to grass in the front and getting one of those new organically correct self-propelled mowers.

It's called a goat.

A Loaf of Bread,
a Jar of Squid, and *Usted*

One of the sure ways to iden-
tify an American tourist (besides the ludicrous way he
sniffs his food before eating it, like a poodle, and this
smug assumption that everywhere is exactly the same as
back home, so he asks, *"Donde esta* Circuit City?"*)* is to
watch the expression on his face as he attempts to use
currency. Americans are enchanted but totally flummoxed
by other countries' money. They love the fact that the bills
come in different colors—a $1-type bill may be blue, a $5
red, a $10 orange—and are gaily decorated with pictures
of kings, queens, and sometimes machinery or farm
animals. (My friend Gino has a theory that the more
obscure the nation is, the more ornate and eccentric is its
money, and so he believes São Tomé has 3-D bills with
holograms of a 1976 Dodge station wagon.)

The problem with foreign currency is the coins. Spain, for example, has at least 325 different coins, ranging in size from a toenail clipping to a baked potato. At any given time I might be carrying between 72¢ and $6,000 in coins, and I have no clue. Travelers habitually store loose coins in hotel ashtrays. There are so many coins in Spain that if you stay in a no-smoking room, you have to ask room service to send up a soup tureen.

The other way you can be sure a tourist is American is by the way he buys a small item at a store. It doesn't matter how fluent he is in the language, or how clearly the coins are marked. When the cashier asks for the money for the purchase, Americans remove all of their coins from their pockets and hold them out like a religious offering. Every transaction is done completely on trust. The cashier could take $48 out of your hand for a pack of cigarettes, and you wouldn't know the difference. Foreign coins are the Rosetta stone of international travel.

In conclusion, let's go over some of the basic rules for staying healthy in a foreign country:

When you are in a foreign airport, never, under any circumstances, make a smart-aleck remark about "a bomba in my bag-o." While you may momentarily enjoy the cheap laugh you get from your traveling companion, it won't seem so funny the next morning in Turkish prison-o.

Don't even think about crossing the street at a busy intersection, even with the light. The traffic will not stop.

You may think you are safe within the crosswalk. How quaint.

Don't attempt to use a pay phone. The number you're dialing—which you've been assured is for one of the finest restaurants in town—will turn out to be somewhere in Holland, and you'll wind up depositing all your coins (you just shove them into the different slots hoping eventually you'll come up with the right combination) to hear someone speaking Dutch.

Remember to put tags on all your luggage so that the people who steal them will know whose clothing they are wearing.

Bon voyage.

Mr. President, I Exhume?

My nephew came back from college the other week declaring his intention to become a presidential scholar. Even as a small boy he'd been fascinated by the presidents, collecting presidential coins, memorizing the birth dates and hometowns.

"So, you'll major in history?" I asked.

"No, grave robbing."

That's the nub of the presidential curriculum these days. First we examine him. Then we exhume him. They've already exhumed Zachary Taylor, whom you may remember from his twenty minutes as president in the nineteenth century. And they want to do the same with Abraham Lincoln. They're getting quite literal about reviewing the body of a man's work.

With Taylor, the idea is to see if he was poisoned. For the past 141 years it has been accepted that Taylor died as a result of eating tainted fruit at a Fourth of July parade. Death by cherries. (As they say in *This Is Spinal Tap* about the drummer who spontaneously combusted, "It happens all the time. It just goes unreported.") Then came the bright idea that Taylor's political enemies had laced the cherries with arsenic. Over the protests of some—including the author of *The Presidencies of Zachary Taylor and Millard Fillmore* (see author's prior book: *The Polyps of Marco Polo's Uncle Larry*)—they dug him up to check.

Honestly, what's the big deal? The guy's been dead for 141 years. Who cares how he died? Let's say they discover he was pecked to death by a duck. What's it to ya? Will it make your spouse any more attractive?

If it turns out he was poisoned—and it wasn't just another life snuffed out by the menace of fresh fruit ("Stay away from those peaches, boys, they'll turn on you like a snake in a sandbox")—historians may begin speculating, "But what if he had lived?" Please. What would he have done, opened up a disco? *Zachary* Taylor is just not that big a deal. Liz? Sure. Lawrence? By all means. Zach? Ehhhh. Leave the poor guy alone. (David Letterman listed the Top 10 things we might discover by exhuming Zachary Taylor. My favorite was: "Oops, he's still alive.")

Lincoln is a big deal. They want to see if he had something called Marfan's syndrome. Again, I say, so what if he did? If people with Marfan's syndrome will be comforted by thinking that a big kahuna like Lincoln had what they've got, *tell* them he had it. I tell my Aunt Bernice that Madonna has hemorrhoids. What's the harm?

Is this where we're going as a culture? Are we going to dig up everybody to see who got poisoned and who had Marfan's syndrome? ("How about Garfield?" "You want to dig up a dead *cat*?") Where will it stop? With mumps? With a sore hamstring? With *zits*? "DNA tests conducted after a recent exhumation of Martin Van Buren revealed he had acne. Historians believe they've finally unlocked the secret of why he grew those preposterous mutton chops." Let's say they decide to exhume Jimmy Hoffa. They'll have to strip-mine half of North America to find him.

In the '70s it was leisure suits. In the '80s it was hostile takeovers. In the '90s it's exhumations? Does this mean if they remake the Mickey Rooney–Judy Garland movies, we'll hear someone say, "Hey kids, I've got a great idea: Let's go out behind the barn and dig up Hitler!"

I suppose it's good news for practical jokers. They can anticipate the next celebrity exhumation, visit the grave one night, and revise history. I mean, let's say some historian got permission to dig up William Howard Taft, and when they opened the coffin, they found Taft with a noose around his neck and a baseball stuffed in his mouth. Or what if they found Big Willy in a strapless evening gown? Wouldn't that be an eye-opener?

(Memo to would-be pranksters: Lincoln is next. Wouldn't it be *great* if the headlines the next day read, LINCOLN WAS SMALL ESKIMO WOMAN, DNA TEST REVEALS.)

Exhumation might also give rise to a new cottage industry: crypt security. You could sell people on the idea of being interred with a live bomb rigged to detonate if the coffin lid is disturbed. This would be called the science of "embombing." (Imagine a group of mourners gathered around a grave, when suddenly they're startled to hear a loud *boom!* "What was *that*?" "Oh that. Teddy Roosevelt. It happens every so often. His heirs have a service contract with General Dynamics."

I see exhumations becoming a craze. I think everyone's going to want to dig someone up. (This could be the death blow for the noble profession of grave robbing, which is a dying field anyway, in a manner of speaking. For centuries grave robbing made sense because folks buried a lot of their personal stuff with them. You could pick up cash, good jewelry, a nice suit. The past few years, what with the recession, cremation, and the decline of the pharaohs, the pickings have been slimmer. These days, *maybe* you get a Timex.)

Now, exhumations will become a part of American life, like "visible panty line" and "pledge week."

Raining on the Weathermen

People on TV talk too much about the weather, and we've got to do something about it. You don't need a weatherman if he's gonna be a windbag.

All we really want to know from the weatherman is this: How hot is it going to be tomorrow, and is it going to rain?

Not the weather today. This is why windows were invented.

Not the weather in Yakima or Europe. Nobody's going to Yakima. And if you're going to Europe, it's not like you're going to cancel because it's drizzling.

Give us a weather forecast for right here.

How hot? Will it rain? Thanks.

This should take three seconds.

The weatherman now has time to tell a quick joke.

Why did the Siamese twins move to England?

Because the other one wanted to drive.

That takes four seconds. Now, some obligatory snappy repartee with the anchor:

"Any chance of a typhoon here by midnight?"

"No."

And that's it. Good-bye. Bring on the sports.

But this isn't what we're getting. Somehow weathermen have become the stars of the newscast. The new technology—the satellite maps, the ability to "put the clouds in motion," and the color radar screen—make a weatherman into the Sharper Image catalog.

In the early days of TV, weather was simple. There was a voluptuous weather girl. Maybe she told you the right weather, maybe she didn't. Weather girls disappeared and were replaced by weather bozos. Weather bozos were middle-aged men who couldn't tell a cumulonimbus cloud from a cowflop but had gimmicks for the forecast. Tex Antoine in New York had a dummy he named Uncle Weatherbee. When it was going to be cold, Antoine put a scarf around Uncle Weatherbee. Weather bozos were great, joyful fun. Willard Scott is a weather bozo, and I say that with all due respect. I admire Willard because he's the least pretentious person on TV. So he isn't sure if it's going to rain this afternoon, so what? Neither am I. In truth, we ask very little from a weatherman: How hot?

Any rain? Do the best you can. We don't get mad when they're wrong—we *expect* them to be wrong. We're very forgiving.

Now, unfortunately, we have meteorologists. They have made weather into a homework assignment. They have one discernible skill—pointing, which does not require four years' postgraduate work. Other than that, it's all hair and atmospheric whim-wham. Who cares where the jet stream is, as long as it isn't coming through your living room. They act like they're inventing the wheel when the truth is they get the same forecast all the other weathermen get from the National Weather Service. They're reading the same maps and coming up with the same predictions. Just once, when all the other guys in town call for "hazy sun, ninety-one to ninety-five degrees," someone ought to take a flyer on "subzero temperatures and hail the size of human skulls."

And why do they preen when it's a nice day? They didn't make the weather. That's as stupid as when they apologize for rain. You don't see Dan Rather apologizing for the invasion of Kuwait.

Meteorology is the ruination of TV weather, just as Rotisserie leagues (and George Will) are the ruination of sports. My colleague Tom Callahan says if he was a weatherman he'd bring a machine on the set, his own private forecasting machine. It'd have whirligigs and doodads and whizbangs that make noises and spin around, and it'd look like what the Wizard of Oz used behind the curtain. Callahan would tell the viewers, "You can look at the other weathermen if you want, but none of them have a machine like this."

Him, I'd watch.

Trou Confessions

You know how when you're leaving on a trip, and you're in somewhat of a rush, and you get in your car and drive off, how you sometimes get the sense that you've forgotten something? And it gnaws at you, because you're *certain* you've forgotten something—but you can't figure out what it is. Wallet? House keys?

Well, former major-league infielder Jose Lind found himself in that position last week. He went out for a drive, and he forgot something.

Who can guess what?

I'll give you a minute.

Okay, who among you guessed? According to the Associated Press, Lind was pulled over by state troopers near

Tampa. Police approached his Toyota Land Cruiser, and inside, they say, they found a gram of cocaine and seven cans of beer. Lind, they said, was "extremely inebriated."

"The reason we didn't do a field sobriety test on the side of the road," trooper Harley Franks reported, "was because he had no pants."

No pants. No underpants. Jose was naked from the waist down.

I wonder what the police said when they read him his rights.

"You have the right to remain silent. You have the right to representation by an attorney. You have the right to call Kuppenheimer . . ."

I hope Lind had the presence of mind to come up with creative excuses for why he might have been driving pantsless. If he was thinking clearly, he could have said:

1. "I'm a professional baseball player, and I do this to toughen my groin for line drives."

2. "I donated my pants to the Police Benevolent Association."

3. "I am indeed wearing pants. Can't you see them? Officer, *have you been drinking*?"

4. "I beg your pardon. I am going to the bathroom, and I would appreciate a little privacy."

5. "Where I come from it is a grievous insult to question a man about the whereabouts of his pants. I'm afraid I'm going to have to demand satisfaction. *En garde!*"

(Actually, this whole thing might work out nicely for Lind. I can see him getting a TV commercial out of this.

There could be a reenactment of the arrest, and Lind steps out of the car—and he's naked except that on his butt is the patch from No Excuses jeans.)

I know what you're thinking: What was *he* thinking?

I myself have gone out of my house without pants; I have run out in a robe or a raincoat early in the morning to pick up the newspaper. Perhaps Mr. Lind did the same thing and then simply forgot he had nothing on but a sweatshirt—because, you know, it's warm in Tampa, and nobody wears a lot of clothes—and he got in his car and . . . this won't work, will it?

No, Jose Lind has entered that rarefied real estate in American cheeseball infamy heretofore occupied only by one Mr. Gerard Finneran, the guy who pooped on the airline beverage cart.

Maybe Jose thought he could get away with it. Maybe he thought nobody would notice. Guys think they are invisible when they are driving their cars, as anyone can attest who has ever seen a guy at a red light excavating a nostril as though it were the catacombs at Halicarnassus.

The other day, immediately after my editor and I expressed disbelief at how someone could actually get into his car and start driving without his pants on, I was walking in the hall, and the first person I saw was my friend Paul— and I emphasize he was the first person I saw. Paul asked me what I was writing about, and I said Jose Lind.

"The ballplayer?" Paul said.

"Right, the ballplayer. He was caught driving around without his pants on!"

"I've done that," Paul said.

"What???"

Then Paul proceeded to tell me about going with his wife and son to the beach at the appropriately named Assateague Island. At the end of the day, while his wife and son used the public shower, Paul decided to play a joke on them. And he got into his car, took off his bathing suit, and started driving around naked.

Ha ha, Paul said. What a riot it was!

I did not say anything.

See, Paul explained enthusiastically, from above the steering wheel he just looked like another beachgoer, so when a cop passed . . .

He paused.

I did not say anything. But I was taking notes.

"Er, this is going to cost me that Cabinet secretary's job, isn't it?" Paul asked.

Uh-huh.

Except in the Jose Lind administration.

Home Is Where the Stomach Is

BARCELONA—There's an old story about a sportswriter who'd been on the road for three solid months, and how he was seen typing into his computer one morning, "My wife's name is Sue. My wife's name is Sue."

And so in that spirit . . . you know you've been away from home too long when:

1. You start sniffing your shirts before deciding which one to wear.

2. You start thinking that the Department of Motor Vehicles is actually a pretty efficient place.

3. You start drinking the water.

4. You call your children and the following conversation takes place:

"Hi kids, it's Daddy."

"Daddy who?"

"What do you mean, 'Daddy who?' Your Daddy. Tony Kornheiser."

"Yes, I recognize the byline."

I have been away for five weeks now. This is too long a period to be gone. I have begun to imagine crazy things, like the potatoes I keep in a bag under the sink have sprouted those horrible little milky yellow pod feet and have given birth to thousands of other potatoes with little milky yellow pod feet, and they've taken over my house—and redecorated. Or that the friends, neighbors, and assorted tradesmen who have the key to my house have started sneaking in to hold Tupperware parties. Or that I've actually won the Publishers Clearing House Sweepstakes, but I wasn't there when Ed McMahon came to personally give me my five million dollars, and he gave it to my neighbors instead, and they immediately moved away, and now gypsies are living in their house and repaving all the driveways on the block.

You know you've been away from home too long when:

You hold your garment bag up to your ear, hoping to hear America.

The hotel cleaning women start looking pretty good. I am continually amazed by the hours the Spanish keep. At three o'clock in the morning on weeknights the cafes are still full, the streets are still jammed. It's so crowded, you'd think Franco was back in town. I've never seen so many people stay up so late. (I guess it's because they take that break during the middle of the day from two to five. You're talking to Spain, and if they put you on hold, pal, you're on *hold.* You know how some offices put Muzak on while you hold? In Spain, you get Ferrante and Teicher's entire career on hold.)

My friend Bill, who lives in Paris, says Spain has the highest incidence of central nervous disorders in Europe, because the people get so little sleep. Bill knows a sixty-two-year-old brain surgeon who lives just like a teenager—he's up drinking and dancing at disco clubs until dawn. "What does he say at last call?" I asked Bill. "Just one more for me, barkeep, and then I've gotta go scrub up"? How'd you like to be this guy's first patient in the morning? How'd you like to be lying on the operating table and hear your brain surgeon say, "Nurse, I may not be that sharp this morning, so when I get to the cerebellum stop me if I do anything crazy. And turn down that light, okay? It's killing me."

You know you've been away from home too long when:

You begin answering questions about your life with the phrase "Where I used to live . . ."

You feel ashamed at how much you have overworked your clothing.

You actually miss mowing your lawn.

You no longer worry about which life-forms expired to create your food, and you no longer consider it odd to see ham being sliced directly off the huge pig leg that hangs in the store window.

Speaking of a hanging pig leg—which is to Spain what nets of Gorgonzola cheese are to Italy, and what the exquisite *Dogs Playing Poker* is to bachelor apartments— reminds me of the fabulous Continente supermarket across the street from the Press Village where I am staying. This is the biggest supermarket I have ever seen. It is 250 yards long and 100 yards deep. The meat department is so far back that by the time you get there, the meat you wanted has spoiled.

The store is laid out so that small, everyday items like tissues are on the extreme left wall, and as you move across the aisles the items get progressively larger, until all the way on the right they are actually selling tractors! Continente is like a chart of the origin of man, all the way from algae to George F. Will. I bring this up because my friend Bill wondered where in Barcelona he could find a copy of Kierkegaard's *Fear and Trembling,* and I told him, "Go to Continente, and take a hard left turn at the chain saws." By the way, they have seventy-five checkout lines, and just like at Peoples, only one was open.

You know you've been away from home for too long when:

You miss Jenny Jones.

You stop noticing how, shall we say, *pungent* so many other people smell, and start wondering if showering is overrated.

You're no longer uncomfortable in a car built for a midget.

You weep with reverie at the thought of an automatic teller machine.

You think of Washington as glamorous and exciting.

Onan the Barbarian

Adolescent boys must be puzzled. First the surgeon general says that to combat the spread of sexually transmitted disease we should consider teaching about masturbation in the schools. ("Finally, a course I can ace!" said my fifteen-year-old nephew.) Then she gets fired for saying it. This raises several important ethical and epistemological questions for the youth of America to ponder:

1. Why do surgeons general dress like such doofuses, with epaulets and chevrons and a chestful of medals? Any minute you expect them to put on a tricorn Napoleon hat, stick a hand in their waistband, and summon their horse.

2. How many immature little euphemisms, like "tickling the tender tamale," will I be able to get away with in this column?

3. Er, just how stupid does Joycelyn Elders think American kids are? (I mean, I know that half of today's American high school students think Luxembourg is in Canada, and the other half think it's a type of cheese. But surely they don't have to be taught, ahem, *this*.)

Actually, as the events of the week proved, Elders's firing had less to do with anything specific she advocated than with the new direction in which Bill Clinton has decided to take the country after great soul-searching and anguished policy reappraisals . . . and a couple of minutes after voters shoved his head into the toilet and flushed. If he were any more of a lame duck, they'd be basting him with orange sauce.

In the tradition of many great historical leaders— O. von Bismarck and A. T. Hun come to mind—Clinton seems suddenly determined to guide the country into a slightly more conservative posture, one that includes orphanages, workhouses, and "publick ducking stools."

When you think about it, Elders was doomed as soon as the election returns came in. She had been a target of the right for a while—hell, she was its biggest fund-raiser; every time she opened her mouth Newt Gingrich heard the cash register rattle. Maybe that's because she had always seemed just the teensiest bit out of the mainstream, such as when she said that we should eat condoms for roughage.

When Clinton had to make an example of someone, she was toast.

What is unfortunately lost in all the politics here is the

very real, serious, important, *fabulously* titillating subject of, ah, "saying hello to Mr. Happy."

Remember all the years of shocking misinformation on this subject, when no one would talk about it, and clergymen intimated that you would go to hell, and your friends told you you would get hairy palms, and there was nowhere to turn for straight information, and you felt like a pervert and you wanted to cry?

Aren't things much better now that a high-ranking government official can calmly and reasonably discuss the subject in public . . . and immediately get her butt fired? (How is it, by the way, that she gets the boot for encouraging safe sex, and Bob Packwood is still here?)

Well, boys and girls, not to worry. Uncle Tony is here to answer all your questions about this subject.

Yes, you in the back.

So, like, I've been told it makes you go blind. Is that true?

That is definitely not true, young man.

I'm a young woman.

Sorry, I don't see so good anymore. Yes?

Could you tell us some more funny terms for it?

Certainly. Smiting the evil bunny, taking Chauncy for a walk, and administering the Heimlich maneuver are but three.

Why are all the surgeons general so weird?

I don't know. I didn't think anyone could be weirder than C. Everett Koop, who wore a little sailor suit and had that peculiar beard without a mustache that made him look like an Amish undertaker, and was as cheerful as a hernia. Doctor? You wouldn't let him take your dog's temperature! Then we got Joycelyn, and she made C. Everett look as normal as Ward Cleaver.

If they did teach this in school, would the classroom teachers teach it?

No. They would bring in specialists to handle it, so to speak.

Specialists? Like who?

Pee-wee Herman.

What would the final exam be?

Don't ask me. I'm still working on how you set up the study hall.

What, in your opinion, would be a great analogy for teaching sex without teaching this particular subject?

Teaching someone to drive without letting him honk the horn.

As a parent, how do you feel about teaching this in school?

I'm concerned that my children might spend too much time doing their homework.

The Flight of
the Bumble

People often ask me, "Tony, why are you afraid to fly?" And I say, "You mean, other than the part about crashing and becoming goo?"

And they say, "Yes, other than that."

So I point to a story like one that ran not long ago in *The Washington Post*. It was on page 1, but as near as I can tell, no one actually read it because it did not have O.J. in the headline. The headline read, U.S. JET BOUND FOR GERMANY MISTAKENLY LANDS IN BELGIUM.

Hmmm.

Without getting too technical, I think it's fair to point out that, geographically, Germany and Belgium are different countries. On most maps of Europe, Germany is in red and Belgium is in green. Couldn't the pilots see that?

The Northwest Airlines jumbo jet out of Detroit was

supposed to land in Frankfurt, but it landed instead in Brussels. You might understand aiming for Miami and hitting Fort Lauderdale, some twenty miles away; in golf we'd call something that close a "gimme." But Brussels and Frankfurt are two hundred miles apart and, not to belabor the point, in technically different political jurisdictions. That's like a dentist extracting the wrong tooth by mistake. Actually, it's more like a dentist extracting your tongue by mistake.

What did they tell these people when they landed in the wrong city?

"On behalf of Northwest, we're sorry, and we'll make it up to you. You can have a free ticket to any of our many destinations—just as long as you don't hold us to a specific one."

Current Northwest slogan: "Some people really know how to fly . . ."

Proposed new Northwest slogan addition: ". . . Now, if only we can teach them where to land."

The best part of this story is that all the cabins have those electronic maps with blinking lights that mark the path and progress of the plane. So the passengers saw the plane wasn't heading to Frankfurt, but they didn't say anything. (I don't blame them. What do you say? "Excuse me, miss, I was just wondering. Is the pilot dead?")

The flight attendants didn't say anything because they thought there might be a hijacker and didn't want to alarm the passengers! (I guess they felt the passengers would be completely at ease just thinking the pilots were going to *a different country* on their own; I mean, I always thought part of the covenant between airline and passenger was the airline would not only land you safely but at a place not far from the terminal where your whole family was waiting for you.) Amazingly, the only people on board who didn't know something was wrong were children under six and the pilots.

Northwest is already conducting an investigation into how this flight could have gone so far astray. At its conclusion a blue-ribbon panel is expected to issue its findings and make a list of recommendations as to how to prevent such an incident from recurring.

(1. Hire only sighted people as pilots. 2. Get rid of those darned electronic maps.)

Giving the pilots the benefit of the doubt, let's remember that they were 35,000 feet in the air, above heavy cloud cover. What do you think they're going to see from there, a sign that says, "Yo, dummkopf, Frankfurt is *that* way"? We're talking about middle-aged men piloting these planes. Everybody knows the eyes go first. Look, I go on my roof, which is 20 feet up, and I can barely see my lawn.

Now, it is true that airplanes have elaborate navigation instruments that can fly and land the planes automatically, without regard to what one sees through one's windshield. But it is best not to get too reliant on these technologies.

A friend of mine said he heard another story from someone in the Federal Aviation Administration, who swears it is true: A couple of hours into a flight from New York to Spain, the pilot left the cockpit to go back and chat up a passenger. The pilot did not return for twenty minutes or so, and by now the copilot needed to go to the bathroom.

The plane was on autopilot anyway, so the copilot used the lavatory in first class. When he returned to the cockpit he found the door was locked. He didn't have a key. He hurriedly located the pilot in the back of the plane, still chatting. The pilot didn't have a key either.

They rounded up the flight attendants, but they also had no keys.

As the story goes, the passengers in first class were then treated to the sight of the pilot of the plane in which they were flying using a fire ax to break into the cockpit.

Anyway, when the Northwest plane landed in Brussels, the pilots had to place that slightly, uh, embarrassing call to the Northwest office in Frankfurt.

What did they say? What excuses did they come up with?

1. It's Tuesday. You know, Belgium.

2. We were confused. *Brussels* has the same number of letters as *Frankfurt,* almost.

3. We're sick of those Frankfurt skinheads beating us up and taking our pilot hats.

4. Love them Belgian waffles.

5. Hey, give us a break, we got the *Europe* part right.

I Scream Sundays

I got a letter the other day from my friend Ben Cohen, the Ben of Ben & Jerry's ice cream. I'm assuming we're friends, since Ben addressed the letter "Dear Friend"—though we've never met, and though I prefer Häagen-Dazs chocolate to any of his politically correct flavors, like Cherry Garcia and Funky Chunky Donkey Meat, the one made out of free-range mule milk.

Ben wrote to solicit clients for Working Assets, a private phone company that will give 1 percent of all your long-distance charges to "environmental and social change groups." The clue that Ben was talking about *liberal* groups came in the next paragraph, which proudly said, "Working Assets is the only phone company that prints its bills on unbleached, 100 percent post-consumer recycled paper."

Most of the other phone companies, I gather, print their bills on paper cut from trees illegally poached from old-growth forests and use ink made from the blood of the spotted owl.

Ben wrote that if I switched over to his telephone company he'd give me sixty free minutes of calls and a pint of ice cream. This is all true. (I'm torn between Anise Joplin, a licorice swirl endorsed by Planned Parenthood, and Great Green Gobs of Greasy Grimy Gopher Guts, a nouveau pistachio.)

I was intrigued by the letter's mention of a "Free Speech Day." On Mondays I could make free calls to targeted political and business leaders and chew them out for some unspeakable act of theirs—like putting iceberg lettuce in a Caesar salad. One of this month's targets is the Florida Citrus Commission, for hiring Rush Limbaugh to hawk orange juice. I guess things must be really slow in the protest movement. I mean, Limbaugh may be a pain in the patootie, but he's not Hitler. What is so terrible about his endorsing citrus fruits? Conservatives should get scurvy? The other target this month is Representative Pat Schroeder. They want her to sponsor a bill to make some guy stop cutting down trees somewhere. I don't care if the call is free, I don't want to talk to Pat Schroeder. In fact, I'll go with any long-distance company that promises me I'll never have to talk to Pat Schroeder. Or Pat Sajak.

Because of my friendship with Ben, I thought about switching over to his company. The brochure said it was the same as the other long-distance companies, with calling cards and twenty-four-hour operators. But I worried: What if my operator was Che Guevara? What if one day I decided I liked school prayer? Would I get all static on my line?

I know what you're thinking: What about *Jerry*? I called Jerry in Vermont, where he supervises the chaining of fifty million pregnant cows to telephone poles, where they are milked with needle-nose pliers and sandpaper. (Just kidding. The cows aren't chained to telephone poles. They're stapled.) I called Jerry. Rob answered. He said, and I'm quoting here: "Jeepers, Tony, Jer's on the road today. Let me get to it. I'm on the prowl for Jer." Jer! Who knew? So Jer calls me. Yep, he's in New York, he gets the message, he calls me. He says he uses Working Assets too. And listen to this. You won't believe it. Ben was in Washington this week, and he didn't even call! Some friend.

The point of all this is the politicization of *everything*.

You pick a phone company based on ideology? I am so out of it. (I picked Sprint because I thought it would help me speed-dial.) This started with credit cards. Because they were all the same, they needed a gimmick. So one offered you a minuscule amount of cash back. And another offered you frequent-flier miles. Another offered you hotel points. And it sort of snowballed. I have a Visa card that earns me points toward a papal indulgence. American Express introduced the concept of "guilty conscience" to charge cards. It promised to make a donation to feed the hungry when you used the card. This let you buy a coat made from the skin of gorilla fetuses and feel as though you were doing something noble.

What's next? If you buy a washer at Sears, could you get them to pledge that the silver-beaked Moluccan scoot frog will be saved from extinction? From now on I'm going to insist that my *dry cleaner* set aside 1 percent of my yearly bills to stop destroying the rain forest. He's got to Save the Ants if He Wants My Pants.

Soon, I see myself going into a luncheonette . . .

"I'd like a tuna sandwich on white toast."

"No tuna. They catch dolphins in those nets. We don't go for that here."

"Okay, a BLT."

"No bacon. You should see how they treat the pigs."

"Okay, just lettuce and tomato."

"No lettuce and tomato. Migrant workers are exploited."

"A cup of coffee, then?"

"Nope. It's from Colombia. Drug cartel."

"Tea?"

"China. Human rights violations."

"I just wanted lunch."

"You should have thought of that when you came in here."

This Will Give You Paws

Today we will examine my friend Gino's ongoing efforts to find a home for a stray puppy. Gino took her home because he is kindhearted, animal-loving, deeply spiritual, warm, benevolent, and something of a moron.

The dog looked bedraggled, with matted, grimy fur, but Gino decided she would be really cute once she was tidied up and her coat was combed out. So he and his family bathed and shampooed the dog until she was squeaky clean. Then they all stood around, looking at her.

"She's the same color she was before, Dad."

"She *can't* be that color. Nothing in nature is that color."

"Maybe certain kinds of phlegm?"

The dog was the color that a white 1964 Chevrolet Impala would be today if it had been parked in the baking sun for thirty years outside a Tijuana bordello. Furthermore, when the fur dried, Gino discovered that the dog's coat had not, in fact, been matted; her fur naturally fell that way. This dog looks as though she has been groomed with pinking shears by a blind man. She doesn't have a coat so much as a Salvation Army sweater.

Also, she has oddly disproportionate dimensions. Her ears belong on one of those giant bats that can negotiate a pitch-black cave strictly by the sense of hearing. You actually expect this dog to emit high-pitched beeps and hang upside down by her tail. Her tail is nearly the length of her body, so she looks like a thirty-pound corn dog on a stick. Come to think of it, she is the exact color of a corn dog. I suspect she was born in Chernobyl.

Gino decided to give the dog away. He figured she would be more attractive to potential owners if he could gin up a pedigree for her. So he posted a picture of the dog on his office wall and invited people to offer their thoughts on what breed it might be. These are the responses he got:

1. "A rare albino Rat-Faced Terrier."
2. "It is not a dog, it is an opossum."
3. "A Shar Pee."
4. "Not sure, but it makes a gerbil look like Rin Tin Tin."

The kindest comment came from my bighearted friend Rita: "It's still a baby," she cooed. "Maybe it will look better soon."

But the truly tragic part is that although this dog can sit on command, that appears to be the extent of her previous training. The puppy had not yet figured out, for example, the difference between "Things to Love and Cherish" and "Things to Go to the Bathroom On."

One day Gino's son called him at work to report that the dog had pooped on the rug.

"Well, that's not so bad," Gino said, a little surprised that his son would call with such mundane news.

"Well, the thing is, Dad, I flushed it down the toilet."

"The dog?"

"No, the poop. But with all those paper towels, it sorta got stuck."

"Are you telling me the toilet is overflowing?"

"Sorta."

"When did it sorta start overflowing?"

"About fifteen minutes ago. *Scooby Doo* was still on."

"IS THERE WATER ALL OVER THE BATHROOM?"

"No."

"Oh, good."

". . . On account of it all rushed out into the dining room. Then it, like, disappeared."

Through this elaborate Socratic method, and by applying elemental formulas of fluid dynamics, Gino calculated that approximately six thousand gallons of poop-infested water had raged from the toilet into his dining room, where it seeped through the floorboards into the drop ceiling of his basement study. The ceiling is now full of puckered brown stains. It looks like the skin of a month-old banana. Gino figures the water is hanging up there like a thundercloud from Hell, waiting for a good moment.

Meanwhile, Gino's other dog, a Labrador retriever named Harry S Truman, has begun to exhibit signs of clinical depression. He mopes around and stays upstairs, where the puppy can't find him. He doesn't even come down for meals. Harry hates the puppy because she spends all her time playfully attempting to bite his privates.

My cynical friend Tammy suggested that Gino name the dog Lorena.

Anyway, two weeks have gone by. The dog now is mostly toilet-trained—and by "mostly" we mean she's doing better than that guy on the airplane—and would make someone a wonderful pet. She's affectionate and obedient. But so far Gino has had no takers, and he's getting desperate. His wife has had it up to here with the dog, and if there's no resolution soon, Gino will be sleeping in my guest room, which I'm not thrilled about, since I've had my heart set on Linda Fiorentino sleeping there. So I have offered to help.

Gino has decided to take out an ad in the paper.

This Will Give You Paws

And being a journalist, he knows he can't publish a lie.

This is how the ad will read:

Free Offer: Autographed Tony Kornheiser memorabilia—includes collected columns, Bandwagon T-shirt, bumper stickers, dog, tote bags, refrigerator magnets . . .

7 3

In Search of Javelin Man

Of all the anxiety-provoking moments of parenting—I'm talking about *before* the little gremlins get their driver's licenses, because afterward there isn't enough Valium in the world to calm you down—but of all the chilling words you can hear as a parent, surely the worst is to pick up the phone and hear:

"This is the school nurse calling . . ."

This actually happened to a New Jersey parent last week. It went something like this:

". . . Now, don't worry, Jeremy will be fine. It missed all his vital organs . . ."

Well, thank God for that. Uh, *what* missed . . . ?

". . . but we had a little trouble getting him into the helicopter to take him to the hospital. We had to saw off six feet of the javelin to fit him through the door."

True story, right down to the saw. Happened to Jeremy Campbell, the fifteen-year-old manager of a New Jersey high school track team. He was speared through the neck by a javelin thrown by another student.

What did he say? "I need this like I need a hole in the head"? (And where did they get the surgeon from, Hechinger?)

By the way, as a sportswriter I need to know this: Did they call the throw a foul? Because if it was legal, counting the distance the javelin covered in the helicopter, it's a world record.

I'm thinking back to high school. Granted, it's been twenty-five years, and times change. But when I think about the things I had to worry about in high school, I list:

1. Nose zits.

2. Charles K. Steinbaum, who had blue veins on his biceps and was displeased by my attentions to his younger sister, Marsha Steinbaum.

3. Solid geometry, particularly the dreaded dodecahedron.

4. The acquisition of beer.

Do you know how far down I'd have to go before I hit "being impaled by a javelin"?

I feel sorry for young Mr. Campbell because of what he is going to have to endure for the rest of his high school life. Every time he walks down the hall, someone will dive for the ground and scream "Incoming!" And just imagine when he arrives at his date's front door, and her dad yells up the stairs, "Hey, Rebecca, the Human Shish Kebab is here. What are you kids gonna do, go *necking*, hahaha?"

THIS IS
WHAT I COME
HOME TO

A Real Turkey of a Weekend

Wednesday, 8 P.M. Just went and picked up my dad at the airport. We're all together for Thanksgiving weekend. There are eleven of us, including my eighty-three-year-old dad, his older brother Gus . . . and Dad's new girlfriend, Tiffany, the Spandex Queen of Fort Lauderdale. Tiffany appears a little young for Dad. I ask her where she was when Kennedy was shot, and she says, "Somebody shot Teddy Kennedy?"

Thursday, 10 A.M. I love this holiday. I love having my whole family around. Oh, my sister Donna assures me that her older boy, Jason, is no serious threat to himself or others this weekend. Two years ago, when he put all our goldfish on a skewer and barbecued them, that was just a sugar rush.

Thursday, 2 P.M. The aroma of the turkey and the stuffing is fabulous! It's a little cramped in the house, but nothing beats the sound of a family laughing together. Donna assures me that that's laughter coming from my daughter's room. "Jason's very careful with the medical kit; he really wants to be a doctor," she says. "That scar on his younger brother Jeremy's neck—Jason was just, well, overzealous. We've changed his diet." I tell my daughter to keep an eye on her new goldfish.

Thursday, 4 P.M. What a joyous feeling, setting the table, lighting the candles, basting the turkey. Tiffany asks me if she can help. I ask if she helps my dad cook. She says, "Oh, Wiggles and I never cook. Except in the spiritual sense." *Wiggles?* Something wiggles at eighty-three.

Thursday, 5 P.M. Dinner is served. I politely ask Tiffany to use a fork.

Thursday, 6 P.M. I probably shouldn't have let Uncle Gus make the punch. I had to drag the kids away from the punch bowl, but I was too late for my brother Steve's wife, Ellen. As she sits in front of six empty cups stacked like Tupperware and starts taking off her clothes, she glowers at Steve and demands to know if "you and your so-called paralegal ever did it on the bathroom floor, so you could see the imprint of our handmade Spanish tiles on her twenty-seven-year-old behind."

Friday, 2 A.M. I shouldn't have put Tiffany in the attic bedroom. *Wiggles* is up there with her. I'm worried about the physical strain. Then again, if she dies, she dies.

A Real Turkey of a Weekend

Friday, 9 A.M. Steve comes in to tell me Ellen had it all wrong. "It's not Spanish tile, it's Italian."

Friday, 11 A.M. I ask the kids why they're not watching the Thanksgiving Day parade reruns on C-SPAN. My daughter says, "Jason has been teaching us about thresholds of pain. . . . Can we build a fire later, Daddy?" Donna, get over here!

Friday, 3 P.M. Uncle Gus gathers all the kids on the kitchen floor and teaches them to spit cranberries in the general direction of the garbage can. He calls this game "Firing Squad." He says: "I'm eighty-five. I can do what I want. Whaddya gonna do, sic Lorena Bobbitt on me?" Actually, I was thinking of gluing him to Jason.

Friday, 6 P.M. I begin marking the liquor levels with masking tape.

Friday, 7 P.M. At dinner Tiffany announces that she feels so comfortable with all of us that she's decided to tell us about her past lives. I think even Dad is surprised to learn that Joan of Arc was a lesbian, and that Robert E. Lee was Jewish.

Saturday, 7 A.M. I'm beginning to get sick of the sound of a family laughing together. I think I prefer the sound of cabs pulling up to take them to the airport.

Saturday, 8 A.M. Over breakfast (turkey pancakes) Jason declares: "It's bloodthirsty, and cruel, to eat a turkey. What would you think if people started cutting up other people and eating them?"

Saturday, noon. Donna asks if I've seen Jeremy in the

past few hours, then adds anxiously, "Uh, Tony, do your children ever take out books on ritualistic sacrifice from the library?"

Saturday, 4 P.M. Steve and Ellen say they have an important announcement. I ask Gus if he has any punch left.

Saturday, 5 P.M. Ellen's ride to the airport shows up.

Saturday, 6 P.M. Steve asks Tiffany if she has a sister.

Saturday, 7 P.M. Is there anything more loathsome than a two-day-old turkey carcass?

Saturday, 8 P.M. Donna says I should rent a video that "the whole family can enjoy." I've got a brother whose wife just left him; a sister whose oldest boy is a sociopath; a drunken, contentious uncle; and a father who's living out an Amy Fisher fantasy. What movie would this whole family enjoy, *Manson Family Values*?

Sunday, 7 A.M. What *shmegegge* invented the four-day weekend?

Sunday, 10 A.M. I catch Gus telling my kids this joke: A man walks into his doctor's office, and the doctor says, "I'm afraid I have bad news for you—you're terminally ill and you have Alzheimer's." So the guy shrugs and says, "At least I'm not terminal."

Sunday, 11 A.M. When are the football games coming on? At least they'll drown out the hideous sound of a family laughing together.

Sunday, 1 P.M. Hey, Dad, don't you think we ought to get an early start on the airport traffic?

Sunday, 2 P.M. No, Steve, you can't move in with me.

A Real Turkey of a Weekend

Sunday, 3 P.M. Donna, one of my neighbors called. She said she hasn't seen her cat in two days.

Sunday, 5 P.M. Kids, promise me. No matter what I say, next year we're going to Taco Bell.

Junkyard Dad

I've just returned from South Florida, where I was visiting my dad. And let me tell you, it was hot.

How hot was it, Tony?

It was so hot—no, wait, let me start again, because you know it's not just the heat, it's the humidity. It's so soupy that when they sell land in South Florida, it's by the bowl! (*Bada-boom.*)

And the mosquitoes! You won't believe how big they are . . . go ahead, ask me.

Okay, but just this once. How big are the mosquitoes in South Florida?

Well, two of them flew into my car, and I was allowed to use the HOV lane. (*Bada-bing.*)

Anyway, I went down there because my dad was in the

hospital; he's getting better, thanks. But while I was there I thought I'd be a good son by tidying up a bit, so I started going through his drawers and closets, and it dawned on me that all these years I'd been living a lie. Here I thought Dad was Ward Cleaver; it turns out he's Fred Sanford.

I mean, junk everywhere.

String in every drawer. Literally hundreds of pieces. In the sock drawer, in the silverware drawer.

I said, "Dad, what's the purpose of all this string?"

He said, "You never know . . ."

You never know what? When a yo-yo tournament is coming to town?

Not just string, but also cigarette lighters from the 1950s and ballpoint pens that don't write but get *schmutz* on your fingers when you click them, and electrical cord and thumbtacks and safety pins, hundreds of them. What could he possibly want with hundreds of safety pins now that the punk-rock craze is over? The man throws out my 1951 Willie Mays rookie card that is now worth eighty thousand dollars and could send my children through college—and he holds on to rolls of masking tape!

And coupons! For an early-bird special where you have to get there by 4 P.M. to get two dollars off some entrée that you wouldn't eat if it were free. For fifty cents off a two-pound jar of Taster's Choice. My dad had twenty-three coupons for Taster's Choice; there's not enough water in the Everglades to brew that much coffee—and that's not counting his coupons that expired in previous *decades*. The kicker is: My dad drinks Folger's! He kept the Taster's

Choice coupons for company. Like who's coming over, Canada?

I love my dad; he's going to be eighty-five next month, God bless him. But at least when my mom was alive she had the sense to throw out most of the junk every few years. Now that he's alone it's like he's become the Fisher King. I'm sure much of my dad's obsessive collecting comes from living through the Great Depression, where he learned to save things and use them again; that might explain why he takes used coffee filters and recycles them as place mats, which grosses out everyone in the family. And it might explain why he has Styrofoam trays—the kind the supermarket puts under chicken parts—stacked up in Doric columns on top of his refrigerator. I tell him he's worried for nothing; these trays automatically come with the food, he'll never run out. But he cleans and saves them anyway. That's from the Depression.

But I'm not from the Depression, and the scary thing visiting my dad made me realize is: I do it too.

I have a matchbook collection. (While my dad was in the hospital I took some of his matches to fill in my own collection; he's legally blind now, so I figure he won't notice. Not only is he legally blind, but the last fifteen years he's been shrinking, so I didn't feel the slightest bit guilty when I threw out all the yellowing recipes from on top of the refrigerator, because as I explained to him, "You can't even *reach* them, let alone see them.") I save sewing kits from hotels, and I don't even sew. I save champagne corks. I must have two hundred stuffed into various drawers; if the Potomac ever overflows, I'll float all the way to Richmond.

Going through my father's drawers and closets was like looking into the future and seeing who I'll be in forty years. In the medicine cabinet I found a comb he's kept since 1973, which urges him to "Vote for Abe Beame," who was running for mayor of New York. I lingered over one drawer where I found thirty-four swizzle sticks! I kept the one from the Copacabana.

Forty years from now my kids will go through my stuff and find the Left Banke album with "Walk Away Renee" and "Pretty Ballerina" on it and wonder what possessed me to save that. Albums and old typewriter ribbons will be my swizzle sticks and string. When I die my children won't have to donate my papers to a museum—everything can go straight into a Dumpster. But there is hope. My friend Nancy tells me she and her pals plan to form a commando squad to keep one another from doing loopy things when they get to be old bags. "We're going to make sneak attacks on each other's homes to make sure nobody has a ball of string in the living room the size of a baby grand, or too many rubber bands wrapped around the doorknobs. And if they start to show up at the bridge table with lipstick that extends their lip lines out to their ears, we're going to march into their homes and say, 'Madge, we're taking away your cosmetics!'"

I look at my father and I worry about my future, so I've given Nancy and her commando squad a list. They'll know it's time to come for me when I start to need a separate drawer for my collection of hotel shoe cloths and a separate drawer for my airline headsets and I begin collecting supermarket plastic bags and stuffing them inside other plastic bags until I have these big blue plastic-bag balloons in my closets. And let's hope they dial 911 if they ever see me put out a used coffee filter as a place mat.

A Daughterly Transition

My daughter left for camp last week. She's thirteen. She is in the middle of what they call the "awkward age" for girls. It's an age where girls are under hormonal attack and tend to fly off the handle at the slightest thing. For example, my daughter recently burst into tears at the sight of me opening up a can of V-8 juice. Some of her friends had just sworn off meats and fish to protest animals being killed for food. My daughter must have felt some peer pressure, since she said, accusingly: "Do you realize how many vegetables have to die for you to quench your thirst?"

The "awkward age" begins at ten and lasts approximately until the end of time.

I was pleased for the opportunity to drive my daughter to the bus stop because I wanted to talk with her about camp. I loved camp—I went for fifteen summers—and I wanted to tell her about what camp was like when I went, back in what she likes to call "the olden days."

She was very enthusiastic about spending this quality time with her good old dad.

And by that I mean she agreed to sit in the car—provided none of her friends actually saw her in the car with *her father;* that would be so embarrassing. I suggested she could lie down in the backseat, and I would drop a blanket over her, and she could pretend she was President Clinton. *(Bada-bing.)*

I think the dilemma of being a thirteen-year-old girl is best summed up by a book I've heard about, titled something like *I Hate You and I Wish You Would Die, but First Can You Drive Me to the Mall?*

Anyway, she sat in the car with me and listened as I yammered on and on about camp and how great it was. I went to Camp Keeyumah in northeastern Pennsylvania. So many of the camps used Indian words, like Lohikan and Chen-A-Wanda. The owners wisely chose to name the camps after Indians rather than after themselves, sparing us names like Camp Krefsky and Camp Mermelstein.

My parents sent me onto the bus with a canteen and a flashlight; none of the kids were even allowed to bring a transistor radio. We were supposed to be "roughing it." The function of camp (other than enabling your parents to finally have sex) was to teach you how to get along without material possessions. Nowadays, kids take so much stuff they should be met at the camp by redcaps. The girls in my daughter's bunk have Walkmans, Discmans, Watchmans, computers, microwaves. Their idea of roughing it is doing without speed dial.

When I was thirteen, I looked forward to the twice-a-week socials with the girls' camp. We always knew when it was a social night, because we'd see the girls walk to the mess hall with their hair rolled high in curlers and covered with rubberized shower caps that were attached by nozzles to portable hair dryers the size of a briefcase. The air would flow in, the shower cap would fill up, and the girl's head would look like a balloon ready to take off over the English Channel for France. Each time I see one of those "photos" in the *Star* or *Enquirer* of a bulb-headed alien landing on the White House lawn, I think of Camp Keeyumah girls on social nights.

On these nights, we boys doused ourselves in Aqua Velva; Red Adair didn't use this much spray to cap the oil fires in Kuwait. Aqua Velva is so strong that when we put it on in the summer of 1961, Yuri Gagarin could have smelled us. What a sight we must have been, with our Ricky Nelson spit curls and fuzzy mohair sweaters, reeking like French whores, deliberately counting out the one-two-three of the box step as we slow-danced with the girls and tried to breathe furtively into their ears the way our counselors taught us.

I told my daughter all this, and I know she was hanging on my every word, because she said: "Could you turn on the radio?"

How about oldies, I said.

"No oldies," she said. "Oldies are for babies."

Just six months ago she loved oldies. Oldies are my music; I felt so connected to her when she gleefully sang along with the Beach Boys.

I saw a change coming a couple of months back when my daughter started singing along with Coolio. Coolio is a rapper whose hair is done in braids that look like the rabbit ears on a 1962 Magnavox.

"You know this song?" I asked her, incredulous.

"Yeah, it's great," she said.

I listened all the way through, and I couldn't understand much. I thought I heard somebody rhyme "is everybody happy" with "Muammar Qaddafi." And I recalled how in "Eve of Destruction" Barry McGuire rhymed "My blood's so mad, feels like coagulatin'" with "I'm sitting here just contemplatin'." At the time I thought it was brilliant, and I was upset when my father heard it and snickered.

That's how kids begin to separate from their parents— through music. The first time I saw Jerry Lee Lewis standing over the piano, shaking his behind and his blond hair, I knew he was for me, and my parents could have Eddie Fisher. Coolio was her Jerry Lee. Coolio! What would she listen to when she was my age, *classic rap?*

I thought of that as my daughter fiddled with the car radio, trying to find hip-hop as we drove to the place where the bus would pick her up for camp. Eight weeks of summer would pass until I saw her again. Did they even have socials where she was going? Did the boys still smother themselves in cologne?

"Is it okay if you kiss me good-bye in the car, Dad?" my daughter said with some hesitancy. "Not right by the bus? It's not that I don't love you, it's, uh . . ."

I understand.

Uncle Boots, Bon Vivant

Uncle Boots is in what they optimistically call a convalescent home in San Francisco. He's not convalescing, though. The last time I saw him, he said he didn't think he'd last the year. "My doctor thinks it's Parkinson's," he sneered, unconfident of the diagnosis. "Whatever it is, it's taken hold of me at a terrible rate."

In recent years, before he moved to San Francisco from Beverly Hills, Boots had trouble with his legs. They hurt when he walked, so he walked slowly, with his feet spread wide, as if trying to balance himself on an unsteady ship. The doctor in L.A. said Boots had phlebitis. In recent months, though, his pain was so severe he couldn't walk at all, not even with a walker. He had a first-floor apartment, fourteen steps to the street. He couldn't climb them. He was trapped, a humiliating experience.

"I've got to get a wheelchair," he said.

"How are you eating?" I asked.

"They deliver," he said.

I looked in the kitchen. There was an open box of corn-flakes in the pantry, a half pint of milk in the refrigerator, and a pot of coffee on the counter. Nothing more.

"Bring me a cup of coffee, will you?" Boots asked.

It rattled in his hand, and he placed it on a table.

"I have to go to a home," he said.

I nodded. "Do you want to?"

"No. But I have to."

"Maybe it won't be so bad," I offered.

He smiled, thanking me for my sweet lie. "Yes, maybe."

What you have to understand is that Boots isn't angry. He'll play the hand he's dealt. He always has. He's been playing with the house's money for years.

Uncle Boots is seventy-five. In his life he loved many women and married two. He is the prodigal son in my family, the rebel, the romantic. He left home young and bummed around; legend says he lived and worked in all forty-eight states. Undoubtedly, he lived over his head in each one of them. He had the kind of taste that once inspired Edward Bennett Williams to say of George Allen: "I gave him an unlimited expense account, and he exceeded it."

Boots told people he was "in foundations." What that meant was he sold bras and girdles. He was a traveling salesman, working the West Coast, a sophisticate and a schmoozer—an unbeatable combination. He settled in

Beverly Hills thirty years ago, renting a stunning duplex one block south of Wilshire, two blocks west of Rodeo. His best friends were bartenders and maître d's; they knew him from San Diego to Seattle. Though he was a grand cook, Boots preferred going out on the town; all I ever remember seeing in his refrigerator were tins of caviar and splits of champagne. He was the most generous man. When you were with him, it was always his treat. The glitzier, the better. Hooray for Hollywood. Boots's show-stopper was ordering without looking at the menu, as if he and the chef had a private understanding. He'd smoke and drink and wink and ask, "Are you having fun?" And yes, you always were.

Once I flew to L.A. to see a man about a movie script. To impress me the man booked lunch at Ma Maison, then the trendiest restaurant in town. Ma Maison was so exclusive it had an unlisted telephone number. In the middle of lunch a waiter brought a telephone to the table and said, "Mr. Kornheiser? For you." It was Boots. He told me to play it cool—he'd called because he knew it'd impress the movie man, and it might help me cut a deal. "Are you having fun?" Boots asked with a wink in his voice, and hung up.

On Thanksgiving, it's Boots I'll think of first. Just before we sit down to eat, I'll open a bottle of liquor, pour a worthy shot in his honor; "To Boots," I'll say, and throw it down like a Michael Jordan dunk. My fondest wish is that he'll be doing the same.

They have a rule against drinking in the convalescent home. It's a bad rule for a serious bourbon man. Remember that terrific barroom scene in *Raiders of the Lost Ark,* where Marian Ravenswood drinks the Tartar under the table? Boots wouldn't have dropped so easily.

I've seen him drunk, but I've never seen him sloppy. Alone, as he is now, a widower, childless, his family scattered to the winds, the bourbon is his most dependable pleasure.

What's the point of taking it away from him?

What are they saving him from? The worst thing about these homes, about growing dependent, is the paternalism. What are they afraid of—that you'll die a month sooner? The main thing they accomplish with their control is the erosion of your spirit.

"They letting you drink?" I asked.

"One a day," he said, laughing slightly. "They've bent the rules for me."

"If I was out there, I'd smuggle you in some bottles."

"Maybe you could send some miniatures," Boots said.

Unfortunately, the post office advises that it is illegal to mail alcoholic beverages. So the best I can do is send my father, Boots's older brother, to San Francisco with all the bourbon he can strap under his coat.

When he gets there, I'll give them enough time to knock back a few while they reminisce about their sunlit youth, and then I'll call and ask my Uncle Boots, "Are you having fun?"

Up Creek,
No Paddle

My son wanted all of us to go canoeing. He'd learned to canoe this summer at camp, and he thought we should do it as a family. You know: The family that canoes together . . . uh, shampoos together.

"Why should we canoe?" I asked him.

"Because the Indians did it," he said.

"The Indians also sold Manhattan island for twenty-four dollars' worth of crap. If you want us to be more like the Indians, should I put our house on the market and say the asking price is a grilled cheese sandwich?"

"There you go again, Dad, reducing everything to a cultural stereotype for a cheap laugh. I want us to canoe because canoeing resonates with the purity of the primitive wilderness. It's an ancient example of coexisting with nature in its most bucolic form."

Up Creek, No Paddle

(Okay, you got me. My son didn't say that—William F. Buckley's son may have said that. My son is nine, and he thinks "bucolic" is a green vegetable. My son doesn't even *listen* to me when I talk to him, let alone answer. I started to talk to him about canoeing, and while I was in the middle of a sentence he walked out of the room to go watch *The Simpsons.*)

Anyway, I'd seen photographs of people canoeing, gliding easily along the water, smiling, having a swell time. These photographs, of course, were in brochures from companies that charge you money to rent their canoes. But I said sure, let's go canoeing.

So we went to Vermont, to the Battenkill River, and rented two canoes. We put on our life jackets, heartily grabbed our paddles—"big end in the water," they told me—and we were off!

At this point I probably should inform you that:

1. I had never canoed before.

2. I can't swim.

These facts become significant later.

There is a general rule that canoeists are urged to follow. Big person in the back, providing power; smaller person in the front, watching for rocks. This works fine if the big person is the size of, say, Cal Ripken, Jr., and the smaller person is the size of, say, Cal Ripken, Sr. But where there is a greater disparity between the two, bad things happen, as I discovered when I was the power stroker and my son was the rock watcher.

I weigh in at 205 pounds, and that's stark naked, and

only if I have recently trimmed my toenails. My son is 60 pounds soaking wet (which he was at the time).

I'm so much heavier, his end of the canoe is basically out of the water; he may as well be a figurehead on the prow. And because I'm so much stronger than he is, my paddling dominates our movement—it was like we had this car and we'd mounted a one-thousand-horsepower hemi engine in the back . . . and a roller skate in the front. My son couldn't really do much except scream that I was heading us for the rocks—again! It was less like a canoe ride and more like Mr. Toad's Wild Ride.

We were paddling smoothly for a while. I got to feeling so damned bucolic that I took off my shoes and hung my legs over the side of the canoe like a real yabbo.

At that point my daughter, who had agreed to suffer through canoeing with us for two hours in exchange for a commitment to spend the next three days in an outlet mall, yelled at me, "Dad, get your feet in the boat and put your shoes back on."

"Excuse me," I said, "but who died and named you Captain Stubing?"

Now for the good part: Because of the drought, the river is down. By that I mean there are stretches where it becomes very difficult to canoe because there is no water; the river is dried up, and you are on land. I am not an expert in topography, but it is my guess that the Battenkill is not technically a river at that point—it is Yemen. You have to pick the canoe up and walk it, or get out and push it, like a sled. Joke: When is a canoe like a dog with no legs, smoking a cigarette? When you take it out for a drag. Hahaha.

Anyway, this happened quite a bit. We were stuck a lot. The first time it happened, I stood up to get out of the canoe, to shove it forward.

"Don't get out of the boat," my daughter screamed.

I laughed, assuming my daughter was expressing the overcautiousness typical of her gender. I spotted a nice-size rock near the surface of the water to balance myself on, and I placed my now-bare foot on it—forgetting that the rock had been worn smooth by, oh, two hundred thousand years of running water. Stepping on that rock was virtually the same as stepping on a bar of soap coated with motor oil and sprinkled with ball bearings. I flew into the air like a cartoon character slipping on a banana peel and fell right on my big fat *tuchus,* causing my family to laugh uproariously, like I'm sure they would have laughed if they'd been lucky enough to see me dismembered in a train wreck. So now I am lying on my back, floundering there like a turtle, splattered with mud, humiliated beyond words, fortunate that there wasn't even enough water in this river to dunk a beer can or I'd have drowned, because, remember, I can't swim.

I got back in the canoe and we paddled the rest of the way. It turned out to be just a short stop. Like Cal Ripken, Jr.

Halftime at the Dog Bowl: K 9, Tony 0

I gave up on growing real tomatoes this year. Instead, I planted those tiny, sissy cherry tomatoes. Not that I'd want to eat the little boogers. It's like eating an eyeball.

Still, I took great pride in my crop. The first one was coming ripe the other day. I had been watching it for weeks, plotting its maturity, watching it turn from the color of a grape to the color of a giant blood blister, waiting for the perfect day to harvest it and throw it at my smug neighbor Arnie, who always grows great tomatoes and belittles mine. Anyway, it was my first tomato of the season. I was so proud. On the perfect day of ripeness, harvest day, I insisted everyone come outside and adore the tomato with me. But when I got to the tomato plant, the ripe one was gone.

Where could it possibly be? I looked around frantically. No tomato. Just my new puppy, Maggie. She . . . had . . . tomato breath.

I've just about had it with this dog. I can't leave her outside because she digs holes in the lawn; my yard now has more pits than a free-range cherry pie. Nor can I leave her inside, because she's up on the furniture, the counter-tops, or the beds. I bought this sour apple stuff to spray around the house to keep her out of certain rooms and off the furniture. It was guaranteed to work. It does, but not on the dog. I hate the smell so much that *I* now sleep on the floor in the kitchen.

Since I'm the first person she sees each day and I'm the one who feeds her, Maggie loves me. And every time I come home from work she is so happy that she pees. (Often on my shoes and pants; I'm one of the few men in my neighborhood who shine their shoes with Resolve carpet cleaner.)

Since I don't want her to pee on the floor, I've devised a routine for when I come home: I step quietly into the family room so as not to tip her off that I'm home. Then I call, "Hi, Maggie!" Then I sprint for the front door, hoping to get outside before she catches me and lets loose. So far it's worked, because Maggie can't negotiate the hairpin turn from the countertop area into the hallway; her feet slide out from under, and momentum thuds her into the refrigerator. Every time. Her knowledge of basic physics is pathetic. (Then again, she probably thinks my knowledge of sniffing butts is pathetic.) If she ever gets good traction, like if they start making the Pump for dogs, she'll catch me in the living room, and then it's good-bye to the rug.

The breeder told me that Maggie has determined that I'm the head of the house, the Big Dog, as it were, and she pees to show her subservience. That's sweet. But couldn't she simply turn down my bed and leave a chocolate on the pillow?

Maggie is a Brittany. That's like a beagle with béarnaise sauce. You're probably curious why I didn't get a golden retriever like everyone else. It's because I didn't want to spring for the bandanna and the Frisbee.

In the first few weeks I had Maggie, I noticed that four or five times each day she would go completely berserk for forty minutes or so—chase her tail, shred tissues, leap into the air and try to spear birds. (She often succeeds in swallowing fireflies, then later coughs them up, and they come out like miners' lights.) This struck me as somewhat unusual for a domestic animal, so I asked someone down the block who has a Brittany what this was about, and she said matter-of-factly, "Oh, that's cocktail hour."

Cocktail hour?

"Yes, four or five times a day for eight or nine years, your dog will go insane. Act like Pauly Shore on amphetamines. Eventually she will outgrow it, around the time she gets gum disease and dies."

I'm used to it, but I don't like it. Just as I'm used to, but don't like, the fact that she rummages through every wastebasket every day and shreds every piece of paper inside, so we have to pile our wastebaskets on top of toilets and tables now, and it looks as if we're preparing for a flood. I also don't like the fact that she's teething, and apparently will be teething until the millennium. Consequently, I have more puncture marks in my arms and legs than if I'd made love to Tim Allen's tool belt. And I don't like the fact that she climbs on top of the kitchen counter and eats sponges off the sink. But what I don't like most of all is that every time I lose sight of Maggie in the house, she uses the occasion to—how can I put this delicately?— poop like a Gatling gun. They bounce off the rug. Sponges, you know.

I finally had enough of this behavior, and this week I signed Maggie up for obedience training. The cost is $75 per session. (Why is it I have this vision of my dog needing $18,000 of postgraduate obedience school?)

Anyway, the trainer comes to my house, and inside thirty minutes she has Maggie behaving like Alistair Cooke. I couldn't believe it. I didn't know whether to walk my dog or serve her gin and tonic water. Maggie was totally obedient. She sat still, upright as a duchess. I thanked the trainer and told her it was the best seventy-five dollars I ever spent. (East of Sunset Boulevard, I mean.)

I walked her out to her car, and by the time I came back Maggie was up on the countertop with her head in the goldfish bowl, trying to eat the fish.

A Complete
and Turtle Disaster

A few months ago my friends Joel and Barbara were hosting a small dinner party when suddenly Joel looked up and saw his dog, a big, contentious, manipulative, in-your-face standard poodle named Lesley Stahl, running friskily across the yard.

In the dog's mouth was a turtle. The turtle's name was Salami. It was also a pet. It had never been in the dog's mouth before and, as far as Joel knew, was not enjoying its voyage. Turtles are accustomed to moving at somewhat slower speeds, speeds that seldom result in their becoming airborne and covered with dog spit.

This was the turtle that Joel's ten-year-old daughter, Arkansas Sue, had brought home from summer camp. (Yes, I am making up most of the names in this story. The real names are too boring. People don't give cool names to their pets or their children anymore. But that is for another column, in which I disclose the name of my hermit crab, Charles Kornheiser IV.)

As Joel scrambled outside to rescue the turtle, to his horror he heard a crunch that sounded like an eggshell breaking. When he reached the dog and pulled the turtle from its mouth, the reptile showed no sign of life, its head and limbs having withdrawn into the shell. Joel said he would gladly have given the turtle mouth-to-mouth resuscitation, but he couldn't find its mouth.

Turtles present certain other anatomical challenges. For example, Joel never knew if Salami was a boy or a girl. How do you tell? Come to think of it, how do turtles mate? Wouldn't that hard shell pose something of a geometric problem? Do they lay eggs? Can you eat turtle eggs? Do you use turtle eggs to make turtle soup? What if you got a "hare" in your turtle soup? Hahahaha. God, I'm good.

Anyway, Joel interrupted his dinner party and called his vet, and the vet said, "We don't handle exotics." Joel said, "Exotics? It's a turtle, not a showgirl." What is so exotic about a turtle? After all, this is a vet. Vets treat animals, no? It's not like Joel tried to bring in a mutant life-form from Alpha Centauri. Anyway, the vet recommended another vet in Alexandria, a thirty-five-minute ride from Joel's house in Chevy Chase.

Keep in mind that the turtle still hadn't moved, and the dinner was getting cold.

Ah, but little Arkansas Sue had said the magic words, "Oh, please, Daddy!"

So Joel and his friend McGeorge excused themselves, got in the car, and began to drive to Alexandria with a dead turtle.

About twenty minutes into the drive they heard movement. The turtle was alive!

"Let's go back and eat dinner," McGeorge said with relief.

And Joel was ready to turn around. But he said: "What if it dies on the way home? What do I tell my daughter?"

McGeorge proposed that they just fling Salami out the window and tell Arkansas Sue that it had died. Joel was appalled at this suggestion. For one thing, there might be a cop around and they would get cited for littering.

So they arrived at the urban pet hospital. (It was a typical Saturday-night crowd—a couple of drunk and disorderly cats, a few dogs with gunshot wounds.)

Eventually, Joel was called to fill out a patient form. He was okay with name and species, quickly writing "Salami" and "Turtle." But he had trouble with the question asking for "type" of turtle. Joel wrote "Green."

In another thirty minutes—and by now dinner was so cold you could skate on it—Joel was ushered into an examination room, where the vet assured him the turtle would be fine but that they would have to hold it overnight to clean it and to keep it under observation in an aquarium tank with a special heat lamp.

Joel said, "Fine." He was feeling like Saint Francis of Assisi.

Then the vet gave him a bill for $170.

And suddenly Joel felt like Francis the Talking Ass.

How special is this aquarium tank, Joel asked. For $170, Salami could get a room at Embassy Suites and a free breakfast. And how much could it cost to clean a turtle? You dip it in the toilet bowl, and *boom*—it's clean! Throw a little Turtle Wax on it, and it shines! Being a lawyer, Joel also made all sorts of compound-sentence threats.

The vet came back with threats of his own. He said Joel could be prosecuted for having a captive wild animal and endangering it by letting his dog eat it.

"Wild animal!" Joel said in disbelief. "If this is a wild animal, Lamb Chop is a predator."

In the end, the vet agreed to void the bill if Joel agreed to donate the turtle to a wildlife preserve, which, apparently, he was required by law to do anyway. Joel felt terrible. Arkansas Sue cried for days. Barbara's dinner party was ruined.

The moral of the urban tale, of course, is to have boy children. A boy would have long ago lost interest in the turtle. A boy would have voted to throw it out the window and go to Burger King.

Short and Sweet

Last week I went to Florida to visit my dad. My dad isn't as young as he used to be. In fact, at eighty-six, my dad isn't as young as Gabby Hayes used to be.

From time to time I've written about my dad, and how he tends to be obsessive about saving certain things, like the Styrofoam trays that supermarket meat comes in; how he washes them and stacks them by the hundreds in his kitchen—you know, in case there's ever a worldwide Styrofoam meat tray shortage. LIKE YOU COULD GO TO A SUPERMARKET ANYWHERE AND GET A PIECE OF CHICKEN WITHOUT ONE. I'll say, "Dad, what are you planning to *do* with these things?" He'll say, "You never know when they'll come in handy." And I'll say, "You never know when meatballs will come in handy, but you don't put them in the linen closet."

Have I told you about my dad's dishes? No, not the china. The china is all packed up. My dad doesn't use the china. "Who am I entertaining, the king of England?" (I told you he was old.) My dad now proudly serves guests on plastic plates with dividers for meat, potatoes, and vegetables. They're plates he borrowed from the airlines twenty-five and thirty years ago. Last week we ate dinner off "Braniff."

When I stay with my dad I sleep on a foldout sofa that sags alarmingly in the middle, so I'm tucked into a tight U. I feel like Wally Schirra in his *Mercury* capsule.

When you get old, one of the first things to go is your personal thermostat. It's so hot inside my dad's apartment it's like being in Indonesia. I'm waiting for Sukarno to come out of the bathroom in flip-flops with a towel around his head. I'll say, "Dad, why is it so hot in here?" And he'll say, "Hot? I didn't notice that it was hot." This is like not noticing that your hair is on fire. It is so hot his clocks are melting off the wall. He lives in a Dali painting.

Anyway, I hadn't seen my dad in almost a year. And what I noticed this time was how short he'd gotten. Not that he was ever tall to begin with; in his prime he was only five feet six. But now he's five feet tall. And the thing is, he's still wearing the pants he wore when he was five feet six. Except now he pulls them up to right under his armpits.

When he sits down, all you see of his shirt is the collar. "When you get old, your body settles," he said. I said, "Dad, it's a body, not a compost heap."

My dad lives in a retirement condo. You know the place. Women walk through the halls in housecoats. Men walk through the halls in pajama bottoms and bedroom slippers. It looks like a slumber party in a supermarket, except instead of shopping carts, everyone is pushing a walker. There is status to walkers. People look and compare and envy, like kids with designer sneakers. *Oooh, Ethel's got herself a six-wheeler!*

Out at the pool, they blare music continually. Guess what kind? Wrong. Not Tommy Dorsey. It's '60s rock! That's right, it's the stuff their kids—like me!—loved, and they *hated* when it came out. I sat there, among these seventy- and eighty-year-olds sitting like flowerpots, baking in the sun, and I actually heard "In-A-Gadda-Da-Vida" on the PA system. And they play it loud because everybody's going deaf. It makes me think that in thirty years, when I'm sitting around the condo pool in my bathrobe and slippers, I'll be listening to Gangsta Boyzz II Booty Menn.

My dad loves having me visit because I can drive him places. He had to give up his license a few years ago when his eyes got bad. This is true: One day he drove my aunt to the doctor, and on the way he pointed and asked, "Is the light red or green?" You think that's scary? He was pointing to a mailbox.

So I drive him around. Last week he insisted I take him to a particular spice store, because he wanted a small jar of minced onion. This particular spice store was eight miles away. I said, "Why don't we just go to a supermarket? There are about twenty of them between here and your spice store." And he said, "Because I can get a good price at this store, sixty-nine cents." How much can it be at a bad price? This is minced onion, not Chanel No. 5. Safeway won't be selling it for $340 an ounce.

So now I'm going eight miles to save two bits, max. And I'm driving in Florida traffic, which is to say I'm creeping along behind a row of cars driven by people whose heads don't extend over the steering wheels, and they're going five miles an hour. Everything is in slow motion. It's like I'm driving through cream of mushroom soup. I'm burning four dollars' worth of gas to get to this place, and I wanna kill myself. We go in the spice store, which is simply a small grocery. And my dad knows right where the spice rack is, walks over and triumphantly plucks a canister off the shelf, and says, "Okay, let's go."

He is holding a can of shoe polish.

My first morning with my dad I squeeze some grapefruit to make juice. He insists that I take the grapefruit rinds and put them into the disposal and grind them up. But he says, "Don't do it before eight A.M., because it makes a terrible noise, and it will wake people up." It is true, the walls are very thin in his condo. They appear to be made of Zig-Zag papers.

Anyway, I'm impressed that my dad is trying to keep the noise down in consideration of the other residents. So you can imagine my shock the next morning at five-thirty when my father's radio blasts on so loud people in Atlanta's Centennial Park ducked and cringed.

I ran into his room, panicked. "What was *that?*"

"Oh, that's my alarm. It wakes me to music," my dad said.

Remember, it is pitch black outside, still eleven hours before the early bird, and I said, "Why do you need an alarm? Are you going somewhere? You got a date?"

"I like this station," he said.

"What's so special about it that it has to come on at five-thirty?"

"It gives the weather," he said.

It gives the weather? Everything in Florida gives the weather! Every TV station. Every radio station. All you get is weather here. So wherever you're from, you can rest assured that the weather here in Florida is better than where you were. Everything that plugs into a socket gives the weather. I could get a weather report from a hair dryer.

"What could there possibly be about the weather at five-thirty in the morning that interests you?" I asked.

"I like the weather on *this* station," my dad said.

And I grabbed my dad, whom I love with all my life, and hugged him, and stared into his eyes, and he stared into mine, and, speaking with the wisdom of age, he said something that filled me with awe, and affection, and mind-boggling terror.

"You know, Tony," he said, "I think you may be getting a little shorter."

A Maggie Dog Story

You remember my Brittany spaniel, Maggie? She started our relationship by eating and digesting $140 of mine in $20 bills. But that's not the only thing Maggie has eaten. She has eaten sponges and shoe boxes and unopened letters, and she's dug used tissues out of the garbage and consumed them as though they were rare Alsatian bonbons. One of her favorite maneuvers is jumping onto the table while the family is eating—she has a vertical leap like Michael Jordan's—and grabbing my napkin and taking it into the living room and shredding it. And when I follow her in there to pick up the pieces, she doubles back to the table and snatches my lamb chop and wolfs it down. She has dug craters in the backyard the size of missile silos. She's routinely pooped in the house.

A Maggie Dog Story

Maggie, the Katzenjammer Dog.

A few weeks ago, I decided to do something about it. I made her into a throw rug.

No, that would have been cruel to the dog. Instead, I was cruel to myself. Some rich, social-climbing interior decorators I know recommended a canine-training facility, a rustic place deep in the woods costing $500 a week, apparently the Phillips Andover of dog-boarding academies. (Upon graduation you go straight to the University of California at Barkley.)

I dropped Maggie off. One week passed, then two, then three. No word from the trainer.

I telephoned.

"It's taking a little longer than I thought," he said. "I found out she is a Brittany, and they are very difficult dogs to train."

He found out she was a Brittany? What did he think she was, an aardvark? He is a professional dog trainer. This is like a master chef suddenly discovering that the potato he had baked and served with sour cream and chives was in fact a banana.

"Another week then?" I asked.

"Maybe," he said. "I'm under a lot of stress," he said.

How much stress can there be teaching a dog not to eat a sponge? It's not like I handed him my dog and said, "Teach her to play the violin."

I waited a week. Then another. Our home was quiet, tranquil, Maggie-free. My kids had nearly forgotten what she looked like. I considered leaving her at the trainer's for good, and bringing home a gerbil, and telling the kids it was Maggie.

Six full weeks passed. In a sense the joke was on Maggie, because at this rate there'd be no money left to eat when she got back.

I called the trainer. "I assume she's trained."

There was a pause. "It's not as much whether the dog is trained," he said, "as whether the family is trained."

"I'm coming to get her right now," I said, and hung up.

The trainer led Maggie out of his house and let her run free. And she ran gloriously. Maggie was fast and sleek and exuberant.

"How will she behave in the house?" I asked.

"Let me show you how good she is in the woods," the trainer said.

And he led us into the woods, with Maggie off the leash. We walked up hills and through valleys. Maggie stayed near, never letting us out of sight—often coming to us, never bolting from us. She actually seemed trained.

"How will she do in the house?" I asked the trainer.

"Let me show you how she does in the road," he said.

The trainer put Maggie on a leash and walked her to the middle of the road that ran by his house, then yanked hard on the leash—flipping Maggie into the air by her neck, like a trout being pulled from a stream. I gasped.

"She won't want to go in the road now," the trainer said.

Of course not—she'll be too busy calling a personal-injury lawyer.

A Maggie Dog Story

Maggie remained on the side of the road, even as we leisurely crossed back and forth.

"How will she do inside the house?" I asked.

"Let me show you how she is in the open field," the trainer said.

And as I watched Maggie perform obediently in the field, I realized that she'd been trained fabulously; she was a great outdoor dog. Which would be fantastic for me—if I were a fur trapper.

"What about in the house?" I asked.

"In the house she stays in a crate," the trainer said.

"I beg your pardon?"

"The object of the training is to make all her rewards come outside," he said. "The reason she's good in the crate is so that you'll reward her by taking her outside."

"She's a house dog. I want her walking around the house, sleeping on the bed with me. I don't want her in a crate. She's not a bowling ball."

"If you don't keep her in a crate, you'll undo all the training," he said.

I piled the kids and dog in the car, and left.

We pulled up to the house. As I opened the door, I tried positive reinforcement. I said, "Maggie, you are a well-trained dog now. You will not revert to your old habits. I have complete confidence in you."

She bounded straight for the kitchen, hopped up on the countertop, and stuck her head in the goldfish bowl.

"No, Maggie!"

This was the magic command. The trainer had assured

me that was all I had to say, and Maggie would instantly shrink, chastened, from what she was doing.

"No!"

She stopped. She looked at me. Then she stuck her paw in the bowl and began to swipe at the goldfish like a bear with a salmon.

That night Maggie ate a napkin. The next night, a sponge. The next night she dashed out the front door and ran into the road. This week she leaped out of the car through a rolled-down window and went bounding through backyards until she fell into a neighbor's swimming pool and had to be fished out, like an old boot.

I am tempted to say that Maggie learned nothing from the dog-training academy, but that would be wrong. Maggie learned one dog skill she'd never had before. Now, without requiring any command from me, entirely on her own initiative, she drinks out of the toilet.

FEAR

OF

FOGEYISM

Bald as I Wanna Be

Last week I got a rare opportunity to be on the TV news. Most of the time when I'm on TV, I'm sitting around with other fat slobs talking about why the strong-side linebacker went into a rotating cover after the tight end showed flex to the weak side. But this time they asked to interview me as an expert on "a question of social consequence." Me, an expert! It was about time. I could not wait to see the videotape afterward, those dignified shots with a close-up of your head, and underneath they give your pedigree, like:

TONY KORNHEISER
Renowned Humorist

or

TONY KORNHEISER
Nationally Syndicated Columnist.

I was going to make a still photo of this shot and send it to friends and relatives. After I saw the videotape, I decided not to. Under my face, this is what it said:

TONY KORNHEISER
Bald Sportswriter.

It was humiliating. Wendy Rieger, the blond bombshell news vixen, was interviewing me about this new pill that would grow hair on bald men. Wow. Who wouldn't want that?

There is just one teensy catch:

It can make you impotent.

Um, doesn't that sort of defeat the whole purpose? Isn't it like curing a hangnail by lopping off your toe?

Being the cagey guy I am, I asked Wendy if the impotence would go away when I stopped taking the pill. Yes, she said. But the newly grown hair would go away as well.

Well, I said, how long is that window of opportunity open? How long before my hair falls out?

She smiled and said kindly, "Don't worry. Not before closing time."

You may have noticed that I have less hair than some men. I mean that in the sense that cactuses have fewer leaves than most plants. Much of my hair is gone. I believe there's a logical explanation for this: I was kidnapped by aliens, who attempted to make me into a topiary French poodle.

Actually, I do not have a receding hairline. I have an advancing skin line. For years I have watched my scalp gradually grow, dislodging the hair on top of my head, like a glacier slowly advancing on a forest—killing the trees, knocking them down like bowling pins and replacing them with cold, smooth ice.

I have a few strands of hair that I sweep up from near my ear and rake across the top of my head. But it hardly covers a thing—my friend Wilbon says, "You look like you're wearing a seat belt across your head."

Anyway, this new pill could be good news for guys like me. Except for the impotence factor. (Of course, if you're already bald and impotent, I guess it's a no-brainer.)

Come on. What kind of Hobson's choice is this? You don't think men want hair on their heads for some idealized idea of appearing handsomer, do you? Men don't care about being handsome for themselves. If there were no women to bag, all men would weigh three hundred pounds, drink out of toilet bowls, and walk around wearing bathrobes all the time, even at formal occasions such as the investiture of the king of England, who would be wearing a bathrobe, too.

"Don't take the pill," Michael Wilbon told me. "Bald is in now."

Bald is in for black guys, I reminded him. Wilbon is bald and black.

"Maybe you could take a pill to get black," he said.

This situation is really unfair to white guys. Bald black guys look really cool, like Michael Jordan. Bald white guys look cool too, but like Frosty the Snowman.

You can tell Frosty is ashamed of what he looks like, because he wears a hat. The only men in the culture who wear hats are firemen, the pope, and bald white guys.

Over the years, I have tried a variety of ways to regain my hair. In my twenties I took shots of estrogen in my scalp. I didn't grow hair—but I went up an entire cup size. In my thirties I bought a toupee. It cost $140. It was curly, like the hair of the father in *The Brady Bunch,* and it sat on top of my own hair like a mushroom cap. I attached it to the sides and back of my head with clips. I wore it once, for about twenty seconds. I walked out of my house, and my neighbor Harvey saw it and started to howl. "Whaddaya got on your head, a duck?" I went back in the house and took it off and never put it on again—except for camouflage, on the night I dismembered Harvey's dog. I'm kidding. I just shaved the dog.

In my early forties I used that sissy-boy Rogaine. My doctor was so sure it would grow hair that he gave me plastic gloves to wear as I applied it so I wouldn't sprout hair on my palms. I used Rogaine for four years, rubbing it on my head twice a day. I'd have done just as well pouring Scotch on my head.

I've never tried transplants, and I think it's a little late in the game now. They like to transplant your own hair from where you have it growing—the only place I can grow hair now is my ears. Ear hair grows straight out, like the bristles of a toothbrush. I would look like Don King, with waxy buildup.

Hair transplants look ridiculous for years until they fill in. You become a Chia Pet that a cow grazed on.

A lot of bald men won't take this pill. I went around the office asking some chrome domes.

Bald as I Wanna Be

Karl is my hero. He is bald and has a ponytail, which takes guts. Talk about flaunting an infirmity. It is like a guy with a speech impediment becoming the Voice of America. Anyway, Karl and a few other baldies said they wouldn't take any medication to regrow their hair even if there weren't the possibility of impotence attached— which sounded like complete denial to me. Joel brought up two interesting points: (1) What if your wife starts buying this pill for you? She wants you to look better and doesn't care if you perform; and (2) after the widespread release of this pill, every man with a thick head of hair will become suspected of being impotent. Women will ask each other, "How did he get that much hair, huh?"

This is an interesting point. From now on, being bald might actually help you nail babes!

Bring on the pill.

Are You Turning into a Fogey?

We had friends over for dinner the other night. It broke up at eleven-thirty. As I walked them to their car, I heard a loud buzzing sound. Looking up the block in the direction of the noise, I was astonished to see about three hundred smooth-cheeked teenagers milling around, brushing up against one another like sex bees doing a mating dance.

Apparently, one of the neighborhood kids had gone to high school that day and announced she was having a party, y'all come. And they all did. Cars were wedged in the entire length of the block, and the kids were swarming in the street. My first thought, which I resisted on the grounds that no one was dead yet, was to call the police. Instead, I retreated inside to listen for automatic-weapon fire. "Look at them," I heard myself saying in my father's voice. "Just *look* at them."

Next morning I went out to assess the damage and was relieved there weren't any chalked body drawings on the sidewalk. There was some broken glass from beer bottles, though. I gingerly scooped up pieces from around my car and put them in a paper bag, and saw my next-door neighbor doing the same.

"I hate to think of myself as a crotchety old man, but it's pretty nervy to throw a large party and not give us some warning," I said.

"You *are* a crotchety old man," he informed me.

And I blushed because he was right. This was one of the early warning signs of fogeyism: thinking about CALLING THE POLICE because KIDS ARE STANDING IN THE STREET. *Just look at them.*

Consider the age-appropriateness of certain words. "Group house," for example. For a young adult, living in a group house is the best of both worlds. You get a high degree of independence from your parents and needed support and familial camaraderie from your housemates. However, a decade or two later if you hear the real estate agent say there's a group house on the block, the first words you think of are "property values." As we get older certain phrases begin to sound more sinister.

Like "small lump."

Like "You really ought to get that looked at."

Like "large parties."

FEAR OF FOGEYISM

I have reached the point where I have begun to look silly in the clothes I like best: old dungarees and T-shirts. You've seen those Bugle Boy ads? I look like an ad for Tuba Man. I am being forced into Fogey-Wear. Lately, I've even started thinking about buying a *bathrobe* and those slippers that slide along the linoleum making a *sqush-sqush* sound that only dogs and Art Linkletter can hear. (By the way, one of the early warning signs of fogeyism is that you no longer care what your underwear looks like. Say it has holes, and the waistband looks like it's been chewed on by a basset hound—so what? You've pretty much given up on the notion that Ali MacGraw is going to drop by the office to play seven minutes in heaven, not that she's still in her prime anyway. See, only a fogey thinks of Ali now. People who care what their underwear looks like are thinking about Sherilyn Fenn dropping by.)

My friend Gene, who's approaching fogeyism—he says he has begun to hear his "body pop . . . I stand up from a chair and I sound like a breakfast cereal"—tells of a conversation he had with his baby-sitter: He asked if she'd heard of Paul McCartney, and she said she'd heard he'd been with a band called Wings. Gene told her he'd been with another band before that. She said she knew that, and if he told her the name she'd recognize it. "The Beatles," Gene said. The baby-sitter said, "That's right. I heard about them on my radio station, because New Kids on the Block just surpassed them in record sales."

(Here's a scary thought: When I'm seventy, my idea of a young chick will be what Bea Arthur looks like now.)

Are You Turning into a Fogey?

The older you get the more your body lets you down. I'm at the stage where I can't lose ten pounds anymore just by skipping lunches. I can't lose ten pounds now without major surgery. You should see what Gene eats for lunch: a grazing salad with enough roughage to unblock the Panama Canal; "roughage," now there's a word that hits home after forty. This is eating? Pale shredded carrots that belong in a crate keeping a VCR from bouncing around, dried olives that look like bat guano, huge leaves of ridged lettuce you suspect is actually manufactured in a chem lab in Romania, and a slab of fish. "I don't want to eat *any* of this," Gene says, "but this fish gives me one and a half hours more of life," if you call this living.

Other early warning signs of fogeyism include:

1. Cruise control.

2. The paralyzing realization that Nolan Ryan is the only professional athlete older than you are, and a postscript at the end of your nightly prayers asking for Ryan's continued good health.

3. Lite rock.

4. Telling your wife, "Don't touch my head."

5. Avoiding mirrors, particularly the one in the dressing room at the pool.

6. Becoming your father, as in: Your children turn on rap music and you say, "You call that garbage music? You can't understand a word they're saying."

7. References to Billy J. Kramer and the Dakotas.

8. Taking the aisle seat instead of the window because it's closer to the bathroom.

9. Conversations about gum disease.

10. Complaining about late-night large-party noise during the ten o'clock news.

11. Saying, "Eat that. There are children starving in The Malvinas."

12. No longer lying to your parents.

13. Lying to your children.

14. Asking for the soft-crusted bread.

15. Keeping your shirt on.

I realize a lot of the early warning signs of fogeyism seem old and trite. That's one of the early warning signs too.

Me Two

The other day I got a funny letter from a person saying that he'd been mistaken for me quite a few times recently. The first time he was standing at a corner when somebody yelled out from a passing automobile on Connecticut Avenue, "Hey, Tony, you da man!" Since then he'd been in restaurants and museums, and he'd seen people staring at him, and he'd heard them whispering the name Tony Kornheiser, a name with which he was initially unfamiliar, except inasmuch as it sounded made-up, and stupid. Like Rootie Kazootie.

He finally understood what was going on when he saw me yakking on some TV talk show.

For a moment, he thought *I* was *him*!

So did his wife.

"She walked in and asked why I hadn't told her I was going to be on TV," he wrote.

He ended his letter saying, "I am now resigned to my fate. I'll never get my fifteen minutes of fame. Judging from your recognition around town, you've already had at least thirty. In the meantime, have you ever been told you remind anyone of a forty-year-old copyright lawyer? Do you have an extra American Express card? Good luck in my career."

You know how everybody has a story of how somebody once said they looked like a particular movie star? In my case it's always Rob Reiner. Story of my life: the spitting image of a big, fat, bald slob, Meathead!

So it was with real trepidation that I called the letter writer, Bruce Joseph, and invited him to lunch at the Palm—figuring even if I didn't get a column out of this, at least I would wangle a fabulous expense-account meal. Ordinarily, the *Post* doesn't spring for big-buck meals; a receipt for any meal that doesn't come in a Styrofoam therm-o-seal box gets scrutinized by *Post* accountants as though it were a letter bomb. But this was personally approved by The Executive Editor, who read Bruce's letter and exclaimed, "Oh my, he looks like *you*! Of course we'll pay for the meal," on the grounds that anyone unfortunate enough to look like me could use a little pampering. Like a last meal for the condemned.

On my way to the restaurant I remembered I'd gone through this once before. Somebody in my neighborhood had said that all his friends swore he and I looked so much alike we could be twins. So I invited him over. When he showed up I was appalled. He looked like a bald Mr. Ed. If I looked like that, I'd either throw myself off a cliff or enter the Belmont Stakes.

And I began to sweat about Bruce Joseph. I didn't know anything about him, except that he was a lawyer. What if he really did look like me? I mean, if he was a dead ringer, he could mess with me. He could misbehave loudly in public places, say, stomping and whistling and demanding that the singer "shake" her "booty" during a Kennedy Center production of *Il Trovatore.* On the other hand, if I was a dead ringer for *him,* I could stroll into a courtroom, peel off a twenty-dollar bill, and say loudly to the bailiff, "Ask His Honor if a few simoleons might help in the furtherance of justice for my client."

So I figured I had a deterrent.

As I reached the glass front door of the restaurant, I stopped to comb those few strands of hair I still have, and a man on the other side opened the door and said with a big grin, "You're not allowed to comb our hair without permission."

I found myself face-to-face with my face!

It was a younger face, more distinguished than mine, and it sat on top of a taller, leaner body—but it was close enough. He kind of looks like I would look if I were a lawyer instead of a doofus.

I had to admit it was a bit eerie.

Bruce told me there was a third look-alike, a prominent gynecologist who Bruce said looked even more like me.

(I can see how looking like a gynecologist could have certain advantages for someone more unscrupulous than myself. I would never impersonate a gynecologist unless I was *certain* I would not be caught, or the Earth was going to explode the next day.)

I asked Bruce how he felt about people thinking he was me.

I was hoping he'd say, "I'm flattered, Mr. Kornheiser, you literary, radio, and TV god! My whole life I was nothing, a total schlepper, until people started mistaking me for you. Now I get good tables at restaurants, good seats at the ball game. Women find me fascinating; they hang on my every word. Men want to hang around with me. I am so happy now, and I owe it all to you, Tony Kornheiser. If you needed a liver transplant, I would shoot myself in the head so you could have mine."

Instead, he said, "My real reaction is that if I had to look like someone recognizable, why couldn't it be Mel Gibson or Tom Cruise? Or Elvis."

A $44.10 lunch—he had the fresh jumbo Maryland crab cakes!—and I had to listen to *that*?

Next thing I know, people will be yelling out of car windows at me, "Hey, Bruce, you da man!"

Close, but No Cigar

Women hate cigars.

You don't have to be Sigmund Freud—a cigar smoker himself—to realize women have panatela envy.

This is because cigars are a Guy Thing. (You can chew them and smoke them. Guys like multipurpose items. This is why guys send away for those gadgets that mix paint and clean fish.)

Like wine, cigars have a connoisseurship. You never see women sitting around talking about a wine's woody flavor or its delightful impertinence. You ask a man what kind of wine he wants, he gives you the varietal, the cask, and the year. You ask a woman, she says, "White." This is why women make good dates.

Women hate not only the aroma of cigars (one woman likened it to "an elephant's foot") but their sociopolitical connotation as well. Women regard cigars as a prime example of the arrogance and self-decreed superiority of men. They consider cigar smoking a hostile act. (Except for my smart friend Martha, who says, "Most men are deadly dull. At least when they're smoking a cigar they seem to resemble something alive a little longer in the evening.")

This is bad, because I've reached the age where I should be smoking cigars, and I can't because American society has turned against them. I feel cheated. I thought when I hit forty, my life would be one fabulous whirl of red meat, brandy, slinky women, and cigars the size of chair legs. (Giving up red meat is one thing, but what the hell happened to slinky women?)

Now, where can you go to smoke a cigar?

1. Your car.

2. Robert Bly's home. (But then you have to smear yourself in mud and animal blood and eat beans and chant something stupid like "Bubba, Bubba, Bubba.")

3. Europe.

Cigar smoking is yet another manly ritual being taken from us men. Like dirty jokes. You can't tell a dirty joke anymore, for fear of coming in third in the New Hampshire primary.

Where are the great cigar smokers now? Churchill, Groucho, Kipling, Milton Berle, Al Capone, George Burns. All either ninety years old or dead.

Not exactly a growth industry.

Close, but No Cigar

Let me close with a joke I just heard. I'm sure you will see how it couldn't be more appropriate to this piece.

A guy from Iowa walks into the lobby bar of the Empire State Building. He sees two men drinking Scotch AND SMOKING CIGARS. He walks over to them and says, "I'm from Iowa, and I'm just amazed at how tall the buildings are in this city!"

One of the men PUTS DOWN HIS CIGAR, winks at his friend, and says, "The amazing thing about these tall buildings is that they're not only masterpieces of architecture, but of aerodynamics. Even if you fall off the roof, you won't hit the ground. You'll fall for a while, but then the air currents will gather beneath you and gently waft you right back up where you fell from."

"You're pulling my leg because you think I am a gullible hick," says the Iowan, who HAS LIT A CIGAR.

"I'll show you," says the New Yorker.

So all three men, CARRYING THEIR CIGARS, go up to the observation deck on the eighty-sixth floor, and the New Yorker jumps off. Down like a shot he goes for seventy-five floors, and then, sure enough, near the bottom, his fall abruptly slows, he stops in midair, and then gently floats back up to the observation deck.

"Amazing," gushes the Iowan.

"You try it," suggests the New Yorker. "Here, I'LL HOLD YOUR CIGAR."

"Okay." And the Iowan leaps off the Empire State Building, and down like a shot he goes for eighty-six floors. No aerodynamic effect. No gentle updraft. *Splattt!* Crushed on the sidewalk like a bug on a windshield.

Up on the observation deck, the second New Yorker takes a sip of his Scotch and a REFLECTIVE PUFF ON HIS CIGAR, and says to his pal, "You sure are a nasty drunk, Superman."

A Clothes Call

I went shopping for nice clothes this week. I rarely do that. I am not a well-dressed man. I dress bad for a sportswriter! That's like being ugly for a hyena. I make Oscar Madison look like Oscar de la Renta.

But in a foolish attempt to upgrade my wardrobe, I went shopping with Michael Wilbon. Wilbon is a snappy dresser. He is so fashionable, he wears four-piece suits. He buys clothes made of buttery fabrics no one ever heard of, like the woven stomach hair of wombat fetuses.

Wilbon took me to a store where he shops, a store so snooty that not only are there no prices displayed, there are no clothes displayed. Basically, you have to request a viewing. We were waited on by a woman so persuasively gorgeous she could have sold sneakers to a flounder. She took me over to a collection of sports jackets, and I tried on something called a Brioni.

"This feels great," I said. "How much is it?"

"It's in the low four figures," she said.

"The what???"

"The low four figures," she said apologetically, as if I should be embarrassed to get such a bargain.

"The last time I got something for the low four figures," I said, "it came with a twelve-month, twelve-thousand-mile guarantee."

I put back the Brioni, and I tried on a jacket that felt like a cloud. "You like Zegna!" Wilbon exclaimed.

I was startled. I looked at the cuff. In ornate script was the name: Ermenegildo Zegna. (Pronounced "Ermenegildo Zegna.") I started to laugh. Armani. Canali. Brioni. Zegna. I pictured four Jewish guys from Queens sitting in a room making up Italian names so they could sell their *shmattes*. I figured Ermenegildo Zegna was probably Murray Steinberg.

"Even I don't have Zegna," Wilbon said, clearly impressed. Ordinarily, nothing impresses Wilbon. If the aurora borealis were lighting up the sky right outside his window, he'd have his head in the refrigerator, hunting for Cheez Whiz.

I looked at the price and gagged. It was more than I had spent for clothes before—I mean, all my clothes combined.

I couldn't believe a sports jacket could cost this much. Surely they'd throw in a few pairs of pants. (I need good pants. A few years ago I had three pairs of pants custom-made for me, at $150 a pair. That was the only time in my life that I spent a bunch of money for nice clothes. The day I picked the pants up I left them in my trunk overnight, and my car was burgled. I gave the police a perfect description of my thief: "a well-dressed man with a thirty-eight-inch waist and thirty-three-inch inseam, wearing taupe." I went out the next day and bought a pair of machine-washable, tumble-dry green chinos for $17.99, and I've never looked back.)

Anyway, I bought the jacket.

"You've made a great purchase," the saleswoman said. "You'll wear this sports jacket for five years," she told me, like this was an eternity.

"Five years? I wear shirts for fifteen."

Wilbon then decided I needed a suit.

I told him I had suits.

"I've seen them," he said. "They look like stuff they give you when you leave prison. When was the last time you bought a suit?"

"You remember *The Bob Newhart Show?*" I said.

"That went off the air six years ago!"

"No, not the one where Bob owns the inn in Vermont. The one where he's married to Suzanne Pleshette."

So we went to another store to buy a suit. Wilbon called ahead. As usual, he knew the salesman. It was like watching the owner of a Las Vegas casino greet Frank Sinatra.

Laid out on a table were five suits under a cardboard sign that actually said, in calligraphy, RESERVED FOR TONY

KORNHEISER. How mortifying. "Why not get a videotape of me picking my nose and put it on *Nightline?*" I said to Wilbon.

All the suits were single-breasted, three-button jobs, like the ones you see the thin twenty-five-year-old models wear in the pages of *Esquire*. I was twenty-five and thin once. I believe at the time Dag Hammarskjöld was UN secretary-general.

You know you are in trouble when you buy an article of clothing in a color that is not technically part of the spectrum. I ended up with a "charcoal ash" suit and a "plum" shirt. At least it was the color of vegetation: Wilbon bought a tie the color of "insouciance."

As soon as I left the store, I started fretting.

The suit was made in Switzerland. Who buys Swiss suits? The Swiss think the height of fashion is lederhosen. The last person my age I saw in a three-button suit was wearing a bozo wig and singing *I Pagliacci*.

I got back to the office, and buyer's anxiety was surging through me like electrical current. I collared the first person I saw and said, "I bought an expensive three-button suit, and I think I made a terrible mistake." He blinked and said, "Why are you talking to me about clothes?"

Good point. I must have been crazy. This was Berko. He writes sports. He dresses like a flood victim.

I went around desperately seeking advice. There were two schools of thought. Some people felt I should not wear a three-button suit because I am too fat and slovenly.

Others, however, disagreed. They felt I should not wear a three-button suit because I am too old and ugly.

Finally I asked David, who edits fashion stories and is a consummate diplomat. He would not opine as to whether I would look good in this suit. He said, "That would be, umm . . . daring." He said it the way you might reluctantly attempt to compliment an author's first novel by saying it "contains many pages."

I took back the suit. The salesman looked at me with contempt. I'm not sure if it is because of my pathetic indecision, or because I was wearing those $17.99 green chinos.

Rolling Back the Clock

About an hour outside of Atlantic City we put on the Rolling Stones tape to get in the mood for the last concert on the Steel Wheels tour. Mike fashioned the tape himself, concentrating on the Stones' early and best years, 1964 through 1970—which, not coincidentally, were our early and best years too. One after another the great garage tunes of our youth rocked the car: "Satisfaction," "Street Fighting Man," "Let's Spend the Night Together," "Gimme Shelter." If you closed your eyes, you almost felt you were alive.

"Remember the first time you heard them?" Mike asked.

I nodded. It was just after the Beatles exploded. At night I listened to WMCA in New York, because they had a disc jockey, B. Mitchell Reid, who played all the British stuff. "It was either 'Not Fade Away' or 'Time Is on My Side.'"

Rolling Back the Clock

"Ti-iii-ime is on my side . . . Yes it is."

"How old were you?" he asked.

"Fifteen."

Mike shook his head and grinned appreciatively. "Same age as Angie is now"—Angie being his daughter.

The car suddenly got so cold I thought my bones froze.

Much as I hate to admit this, ti-iii-ime is not on my side anymore. I went to see the Stones this week knowing that, and hoping they would help me put my finger in the dike for a few hours. They'd worked for me at RFK in September; I'd walked away from that concert imagining I still had hair.

I am of that generation that so worshipped the Rectitude of Youth that not only didn't we like older people, or trust older people, or want anything to do with older people—and by older we meant parents, police, school administrators, politicians, and everyone over thirty except the guy who owned the record store—but we actually adopted as an ideology: "Hope I die before I get old." (And no, the irony isn't lost here that the Who themselves recombined to tour this year, and there were some who thought they should have taken their own advice.)

Old terrorizes us. We do everything we can to prevent growing old. We lead lives of delay. It's called the Peter Pan syndrome. We marry late. We have our babies late. We settle in late and delude ourselves into thinking that the house—God help us, it looks just like our parents' house!—the car, the gardener don't hold our leash; any time we choose, we can chuck it all and be perfectly content pitching a tent in the woods. (Like that isn't truly mental, I must say.)

We have Rogaine.

We have Retin-A.

We have the Abdominizer!

And, however briefly, we still have the Stones to tell us even if we can't always get what we want, if we try sometime, we might find, we can get what we need.

The key to remaining young is to have old entertainers. A forty-year-old could hardly feel young by going to a Guns N' Roses concert. He'd feel so bewildered that he might miss the fact that to this generation of eighteen-year-olds these arrogant, insulting, swaggering tomcats are the Rolling Stones. A forty-year-old rocker has enough ambivalence as it is (have you any idea how rough it is squeezing into these jeans?) not to have to put up with posers. Gimme Mick!

Mick's my age, and if you start him up, he'll never stop. Makes a grown man cry to see how elegantly thin he is, and how he can still prance and strut and pout and sneer; the best sneer in the business, sexy and evil and leering all at the same time—the very face of rock and roll (though you wouldn't want to look too closely at the giant screen, because his age shows in lines as deep as planting rows; the farther back you stand, the better everyone looks.)

"We're gonna play a couple of new songs for you," Mick says. "We can't keep recycling the old ones."

Why not?

It's precisely the old ones that brought us. The old ones,

the ones we know by heart, the ones we danced to all night long, before there was any such thing as a mortgage, or a deadline, or the grim possibility of buying a station wagon.

The older you get, the more it sets in that you're not as empowered as you thought, that like all generations before yours, you'll have to settle for small victories. Seeing the Rolling Stones, verifying they can still rock and roll, is one of those small victories.

"Look at Keith," someone says.

"Looks great for a dead man" is the reply. "You think anybody would've bet the over on Keith, huh? He doesn't even have his own blood."

"And look at Wyman in that stupid red jacket and string tie. He looks like a waiter at an Italian restaurant."

"Yeah, but he's getting one fifth of the money."

Needless to say, I was on my feet through the whole concert, dancing in the aisle, shouting out the words to the songs, pumping my fist into the air at the appropriate time. Then sometime in the middle of "Jumpin' Jack Flash" I glanced over at a couple of middle-aged men trying to keep the beat, retro-rockers, and I was struck by how silly they looked, and how old, until it dawned on me that they weren't any older or any sillier than me, and like me, they'd probably come suspecting this might be the last time they'd feel this good, this young, this free. So for them, and for all of us in this crowded boat, I shook the rafters screaming, "It's a gas, gas, gas!"

Heading for Oblivion

I'd better write fast.

I might not live till the end of this column.

I'm bald, you see.

According to a Boston University study, men who are bald like me—I suffer from a highly technical medical condition sometimes referred to as "Fred Mertz head"— have a 340 percent higher risk of a heart attack than men with a full head of hair. *340 percent!* That alone is enough to give me a heart attack.

The story was front-page in *The New York Times*.

I know, because approximately eighteen thousand people showed it to me. My boss, who has a head of hair like a raccoon, came over to me and with great glee said, "I saved something for you." Then he handed me the newspaper and stood there as proud as if he'd deciphered Avogadro's number, and he shouted out, "Not only do you look bad—*now, you're dead!*" Thank you, Mr. Sensitivity.

Luckily, my friend Nancy was nearby, and she sweetly tried to offer encouragement by reminding me that last year there was a similar report, about how left-handers die young, that has since been discredited. Being a righty, I replied, "Who cares about left-handers?" (I am reminded that a friend approached me about this bald–heart attack business and said, "I have empathy for you, because last week there was a study that prostate cancer is linked to vasectomies, and I've had a vasectomy," and because I'm a caring, compassionate kind of guy, I said, "What does that have to do with *me?*")

So the point is: I'm bald, and any second now I could drop dead. And nobody will even bother with an autopsy—they'll just look at my head and say, "Yeah, it figures." They'll write on the coroner's certificate: "The Mortis Beat the Hair." (Sorry.)

And here I was thinking that I was just *thinning.*

Isn't it great how bald people have so many euphemisms that sugarcoat their condition—like the Eskimos have one thousand words for "snow." Men who have no more hair than a plucked chicken will say they have "a receding hairline" or "a prominent forehead." I like to refer to myself (and millions of other men who have been sentenced to die prematurely) as "follically challenged."

The *Times* story was accompanied by a twelve-picture

graph of the various stages of baldness. Underneath the one that most resembled my head was a caption that read: "Already deceased."

I have male-pattern baldness. I love that phrase, "male-pattern." It makes me sound like a quilt. Excuse me, miss, would it be possible to see something in a slightly thicker weave?

I want to send away to Butterick or Simplicity for a different pattern. My hair began falling out when I was eighteen. I asked my doctor if there was any way I could save it. He said, "Sure," and handed me a Baggie.

I thought the aesthetics of baldness was pain enough. Now I find out it's a double whammy. Damn. Just when baldness was becoming sort of vogue—God bless Michael Jordan.

My smart friend Martha was very insightful about why bald men die early: "I think it's because they're incredibly anxious and angry about being bald—and it kills them."

Ironic, isn't it? For years I have tried to foil my balding genes. I took hormone treatments. (They gave me estrogen. I felt fine, but I had an uncontrollable urge to become attorney general.) I tried Rogaine. But I did it all for vanity's sake—*to get women.* Who knew it was life and death?

If one of these goofy miracle cures works—like the one on the infomercial, where the guy shakes out what looks like herbs on your scalp, then rubs them in, and voilà, your head suddenly looks like it was painted by Earl Scheib—if one of these miracle cures works, and I can really grow hair, will that *save my life?* Because if it will, I'll put a Chia Pet on my head.

I can't believe there's real science here. How can so many bald people die young when they all look so old?

Surely the study must be a mistake. Not all bald people die young. Winston Churchill lived to be 162. George Burns, bald as an egg, and he lived to be 340. Ike. Looked bad, yeah, but lived a long time. Gandhi. Got shot, so we don't know how long he would have gone. Julius Caesar. Stabbed. Ditto. The jury's still out on Sinead O'Connor.

Isn't it interesting that Upjohn, which manufactures Rogaine, sponsored the study? Is this to scare you into using the product as your only hedge against death?

Are we dying from baldness, or exposure?

Do you think maybe if I got a really good *hat* . . . ?

It's Palm Sunday

NEW ORLEANS—became a little concerned about my health this week when I read a story in *USA Today* reporting the results of a scientific study that concluded, and I quote, "Boorish, bigmouth men die younger."

What does this have to do with *me*, you ask?

What a pig-faced moron you are. It has to do with me because even sophisticated, self-effacing men like me must occasionally act a little assertively, such as when the waiter gets my order wrong and it is necessary to express my displeasure via loudly questioning the legitimacy of his birth, jamming bread sticks in his mouth and pulling his pants down.

Anyway, this study got me a little worried. It occurred to me that possibly I should reconsider my attitude and begin to treat people a teensy bit better, harness my temper and arrogance a bit. You know, take up polo. Read Noël Coward. But instead, I decided to seek a second opinion, from another scientific expert who might have a different, less dire, but equally valid view of my mortality. So I went to see a tarot-card reader.

There are loads of them here in the French Quarter, amid the jugglers and the clowns who all do tricks for you. I picked Wyndee, a twenty-three-year-old whose mother works at an adjoining card table reading palms! What a nice touch. A family business. You know what they say: The family that prognosticates together . . . um, eats frogs and grapes together.

Of the many reasons I chose Wyndee, the most important one was that unlike many of her equally qualified colleagues on Jackson Square, she had no obvious boils on her nose. What is it with tarot readers? Why do so many of them look like they've just walked out of a Diane Arbus photo?

"Just tell me this much about my future," I told Wyndee. "Will it involve Elizabeth Hurley?"

For those of you who have never had a tarot reading, let me explain. There is a deck of cards, and the reader turns over ten, and from those ten tells you what's going on in your life now, and what's going to happen to you in the future. They are exactly like TV weathermen, only more accurate.

Wyndee (her sister is named Nynteepercentchance-ofrain) had me shuffle the deck. Then she began flipping cards. (As she turned them over I suppressed an urge to say, "Go fish.") All the cards contain eerie Gothic drawings of a person, each symbolizing a hifalutin concept, like "Hope" or "Beauty" or "A Bridge to the Twenty-first Century."

Wyndee turned a card up.

"Death."

I took this as a bad sign.

She tried to reassure me. "It doesn't mean physical death. Actually, it can be good."

"Good death? Like good cholesterol?" I asked, grasping.

I looked at my other cards and pointed to the one with a man lying on his stomach with ten swords in his back. "That's a *good* card?" I asked. She didn't give me a straight answer. This was not looking fabulous.

Then I saw a card with three swords piercing a heart. "You're going to tell me that's good too, even though it looks like whoever gets that card ought to call Dr. DeBakey?"

Wyndee made her first pronouncement.

"You're an anxious, neurotic person." She was not looking at the cards.

She went on with the reading. I had the King of Cups, which sounded good to me, like a guy who needs a very big athletic supporter. And the Knight of Wands, who also seemed to carry a big stick, if you get my drift, and a Queen. I was hoping it was the Queen of Soul, which of course would mean I command r-e-s-p-e-c-t. The thrust of what it all meant, she said, was that I was in a state of flux, and my career would soon be taking a different direction.

"How soon?" I asked. I was hopeful. Maybe I didn't have to bother writing this column.

Suddenly, Wyndee looked at me and asked, "Are you from New York?"

I am. Now *that* was impressive. "Which cards told you that?"

"Your accent told me that. I lived in Brooklyn once."

Oh.

Things were going so well, I decided to have Wyndee read my palm also. She told me to extend the hand I write with.

I did, and she gasped, "The simian crease!"

She called to her mother. "Mom, read his palm. He has the simian crease."

I was alarmed. The simian crease! I might have to climb up the Empire State Building.

I moved on to Wyndee's mom.

In short order she told me that I was "inflexible, dogmatic, impatient, and self-indulgent—energetically so."

"You got all that from my hand?" I asked her. "Or were you talking to my family?"

"How old are you, forty?" she asked.

Why was she looking at my palm? Couldn't she tell by reading the lines on my face?

"Right," she said. "Closer to fifty."

The simian crease, it turns out, is a big deal. "It occurs," she said, pointing to a straight line across the middle of my palm, "when your head line and your heart line are fused together.

"It's the merging of the mental and the emotional. People who have this search for ideas; they're very forceful and creative. What do you do for a living?"

"I'm a sportswriter."

"Well, that's certainly creative," she said patronizingly.

And suddenly, I realized I had something important to ask her.

"Um, do you see anything in there about taking Green Bay and giving fourteen?"

She looked at me like I was, well, a big ape.

No, I won't tell you what she answered.

It might affect the odds. I need them to stay exactly where they are.

A Stitch in Time

The other day I took my daughter shopping at the mall, and the salesgirl who was showing her some hideous crud-brown nail polish gestured at me and asked, "Will your grandpa let you wear this?"

Right then I decided that the perfect Christmas gift for me was a facelift. According to a story in *The Washington Post,* middle-aged losers like me are turning to plastic surgery so they can stay on pace with all those fresh-faced thirty-year-olds in the office who are trying to steal their jobs. I can get the whole schmear for five grand—eye job, nose job, forehead job. If I act now, maybe they'll throw in a body wax.

Listen, everybody my age is getting one. Nobody wants to face being fifty in the face he's in. The other day I turned on my TV and I saw a familiar newscaster—only she had a new face! There wasn't a wrinkle on her; her skin had been pulled back so taut you could play "Wipe Out" on her cheeks with swizzle sticks. And her eyes were bulging. You know the saying that after a facelift, you don't look younger, you just look perpetually . . . surprised? Well, she didn't look just surprised, she looked like she had been wired to jumper cables. I'm told that when people remark on the difference in her appearance, she says, "I've had my hair lightened." Which would be like my getting a sex-change operation, then telling people, "I, um, got new glasses."

Another TV newscaster also recently got a facelift. I saw him on the set when he came back to work. His skin was so tight and tender that if you were on his side when you were talking to him, he couldn't move his eyes to make contact with you—he had to slowly turn his whole head, like a gun turret. It was like Max Headroom doing the news.

We see ourselves in a mirror every day, so it doesn't occur to us how much we've aged. But when you step back a bit it's frightful. I recently ran into a high school friend whom I hadn't seen in twenty-five years, and I said to myself, "Jeez, this guy looks like somebody Grant Wood painted." And then I could see in his eyes that he was thinking the same thing about me. It's a good thing you see your spouse every day. Because if you didn't see each other for a few years, between, say, thirty-eight and forty-five, and then—*boing!*—there he/she was, you would run screaming from the room like your pants were on fire. That's why travel in the Middle East is so terrifying. It is not simply the prospect of getting taken hostage for five years by the Hezbollah—it's the terror of having to see your spouse after they set you free.

It doesn't surprise me that facelifts are becoming so popular—the number of cosmetic surgeries has more than doubled since 1990, and I don't think Loni Anderson has had them *all*. But Loni does look scary, doesn't she? That's not her face. It's a perfectly nice face, but it doesn't fit on a fifty-year-old woman. It just looks wrong. A giraffe has a perfectly nice head, but it would look ridiculous on a cocker spaniel. They've pulled Loni's skin so far back they've had to tie it in a knot the size of a Mercedes-Benz medallion on the back of her head. God forbid she sneezes violently. Her whole face would collapse like a mudslide.

The allure of facelifts is obvious. Speed and immediacy. This is not like pledging yourself to a two-year diet of rice cakes so you can fit into a pair of pants without a drawstring. A facelift requires no strain, no work on your part. No skin off your nose, so to speak. Unfortunately, speed is also the problem with facelifts. The change is embarrassingly immediate, and extreme. Beforehand, you look like an aging person with some wrinkles, a few laugh lines, a crow's foot or two. But afterward, you look like a puppet. You look exactly like Kukla.

(Speaking of puppets, have you seen Shari Lewis lately?

She must be what, eighty? She still has that mop of orange curls, but her head looks so tight and shrunken you could palm it, like a duckpin bowling ball.)

My friend Nancy, who is roughly my age, says if she ever gets surgery, it will be only on her neck. "I don't want to be one of those women who always wear a scarf, like Barbara Walters," she said. "That's the tip-off. Everybody knows your neck is gone. You've either got a wattle, like a turkey, or three chins."

Nancy thinks women who've had breast implants made a mistake. "Here's the problem: You're eighty years old. You're in a nursing home. You're drooling out of one side of your mouth, and you've got hooters the size of Mount Rushmore. The orderlies are feeding you creamed squash and copping a feel. It's my personal nightmare."

Finally, I told my friend Gino about my plan for a facelift; when you are contemplating a major life decision, it is wise to seek the counsel of a close friend, someone who cares about you but has a perspective that you yourself could not have.

Gino was doubtful. I asked: Is it too risky?

"No," he said. "It is that there are some people who nature has *intended* to be profoundly ugly. You look like a toadstool. Giving you a facelift would be like putting tail fins on a dump truck."

Oh.

The Vision Thing

I am sitting here, holding in my hands an object that has changed my life.

It's a pair of reading glasses my friend Nancy gave to me.

Suddenly, I can hold a typed letter in front of my face and read it without having to stretch my arms out like I'm playing a trombone.

These last few years I'd noticed that it was getting increasingly hard to read books and magazines the way I'd always read them before—in the same room as me.

The only things I could read comfortably were highway signs from about half a mile away. If you reprinted the full text of *One Hundred Years of Solitude* on one of those signs, I could read it—depending on how fast we were moving, of course. The closer I brought anything printed to my face, the more blurred the type became. It was like trying to read Chaucer through a schmear of cream cheese. And it was getting worse. I was completely helpless with small type—like the nutrition label on a soup can. It aggravated me that I wasn't able to keep track of my daily intake of riboflavin.

Last month I bought a watch. When I got it home I noticed it had a small dark spot on the right side of the face that I must have missed in the shop. I rubbed and rubbed it with glass cleaner, but it didn't come out. Then my daughter looked at the watch and told me it wasn't a spot—it was the date.

Nancy came to my rescue when she saw me attempting to type this column with my toes. Handing me a pair of glasses, Nancy explained, "The mature eye has trouble making the adjustment from looking long-range to looking short-range."

The *mature* eye had a ring of euphemism, much like "relaxed-fit jeans," which is what they call jeans designed to fit middle-aged guys built like Mallomars.

I put the glasses on and realized that if I'd been sitting any farther away from my computer at *The Washington Post,* I'd have been at *The New York Times.*

"Wow," I said.

"Keep them," Nancy said. "I have loads of them at home. I keep a pair every place I run into small type—by the cookbooks, the phone books, the VCR. They only cost about twelve dollars a pair."

"Where'd you get them?" I asked.

"The supermarket."

A Vision Thing

Buying a pair of eyeglasses at the supermarket sounds to me like buying a haddock at a gas station, but who am I to complain? For once, I was comfortably reading something smaller than the top *E* on an eye chart. "What do they call these things?" I asked. "Adult-reader acuity-enhancement devices"?

"Old-people glasses," Nancy said.

The thought of wearing "old-people glasses" actually doesn't bother me, since I've recently had extensive cosmetic surgery, and I look fabulous! That's what I told the guy from *Washingtonian* magazine who called me the other day and said, "We got a tip that you had cosmetic surgery over the summer. Did you?"

Well, no, I didn't. But I could tell they wanted it to be true. So I said, "Geez, you got me! I had my eyes done, my chin done, and a blond-hair transplant. Now I look just like Vanna White." I can't wait to see what they print.

I told my friend Gino about my new glasses, and he was delighted. This is not because he loves and respects me as a friend and was happy that I'd found a way to see better, but because he hates and resents me. He has been wearing glasses since he was ten, and he cannot stand people like me who have had perfect eyesight and treat people like him as though they are pitiably disabled, like someone with half a body who rolls around the street on a skateboard.

There is a pecking order among the visually disabled. Gino has bifocals. But he thinks he is *waaay* luckier than his friend, who has *tri*focals. He introduced me to the guy, who is the *Post* arts editor. His name is John Pancake, and Gino asked me not to make fun of John's name, because that would be a cheap shot. Anyway, John's glasses are indeed an amazing thing to behold. They have two deep gouges running across the lenses, like they've been strip-mined. The top third is for driving, the middle third for reading a computer screen, and the bottom third for reading up close. They look weird, but I can "flatly" assure you, and I am not being "flip," that they make John Pancake a much "batter" editor.

Anyway, getting back to my conversation with Gino, we were having lunch in a deli and I was lording it over him about how, unlike him, I still needed glasses only to read, and it was no big deal.

"Oh, yeah?" he sneered, shoving his chopped-liver sandwich right up to my face. "Can you see this?"

I couldn't. I hadn't brought my glasses with me, because I wasn't planning on reading lunch. The sandwich was a big brown blur. It could have been a hamster for all I knew. "What if there was a big, fat, wriggling tapeworm coming right out of the chopped liver?" he said. "Would you see it? Or would you just . . . *eat* it?"

He had a point.

I *hate* the four-eyed geek.

Now I wear my glasses for eating, too.

HE SAID . . .
SHE SAID . . .

Just Desert

As you know, I am fascinated with the way our culture is constantly redefining itself in terms of gender. Consequently, I am continuously searching for empirical tests to measure the differences between men and women.

Today, Test 1: The Desert Island.

Assuming you are stuck on this desert island, who are the five people you'd want with you?

There is one rule: No sex.

(That sound you hear is thousands of grumbling men scratching Claudia Schiffer off their lists.)

Not only is there no sex on this island, but there is no longing for sex, no contemplating sex, no memories of sex. Sex is not part of the equation for whom you would bring to this desert island—a small island in the South

Pacific named, uh, Nonookie Island, overgrown with salt-peter trees.

I went around asking some friends whom they would take to the island. I asked men and women, black and white, in their twenties, thirties, and forties. (Can I help it if there was nobody in their fifties or sixties within ten feet of my desk? Who do I look like, George Gallup?)

I first sought out my friend Nancy, who pondered this inane question as though I had asked her to weigh the epistemological and theological implications of the virgin birth. Nancy opted for utility. To keep herself amused she wanted "a raconteur." To keep herself healthy she wanted "somebody good at knocking fish over the head and cooking them." To keep herself sheltered she wanted "somebody who was good at construction—who specialized in irrigation and plumbing and providing me with hot water." In the hope that she could get off the island, she wanted a communications expert, who could make contact with the outside world. For her last person, she wanted a doctor. All sound, generic choices, I thought.

Would they be men or women, I asked.

"Half and half," Nancy said. Three men, two women. Counting her, an even split.

Then she asked, "What area of specialization would you look for?"

"All guys," I said.

She was dumbstruck. "That's it, just . . . guys? Sitting around scratching yourselves? Twenty years later you'd still be sitting on tree stumps. You wouldn't even have water. We'd have calamari. We'd have built a skiff from birch bark and saplings. We'd be off the island! You'd be sitting around debating the wisdom of the pitching changes in Game Six of the 1986 World Series."

At that point Zsa Zsa walked over. (Zsa Zsa is not her real name. But trust me, it fits.) I sketched out the desert-island question.

Zsa Zsa was less utilitarian than Nancy. "I don't want a desalinization expert," Zsa Zsa said. "I want entertainment."

Ultimately, Zsa Zsa's five also included three men and two women.

"Men never pick women," I said. "If there's no sex, there's no need for women."

"That's sexist and ridiculous," Zsa Zsa said.

"Watch," I said.

We went over to Richard. He rattled off five sportswriters without even looking up from his sandwich.

"No girls at all?" Zsa Zsa asked.

"Whmf fnuh?" Richard said, drooling mayonnaise.

I translated: "What for?"

We went over to Michael Wilbon, the famous columnist and bon vivant.

"No sex on the island?" he asked.

"A nonfactor," I said.

"No babes," he declared. "Only three things matter—sports, money, and sex. If you take away sex, you're down to sports and money. And since you only need money for babes, there are no babes on this trip."

"Pig," Zsa Zsa said.

We went to Gino next. Unlike the other men, Gino is at least semiliterate. He works in another section of the paper. He occasionally attends public events that do not begin with "The Star-Spangled Banner." I popped the question.

"The starting five from the 1972 New York Knicks," Gino said.

"I can't believe this," Zsa Zsa said. "What is with you people?"

"Wait," Gino said. "Maybe that was a little hasty."

"Ah," purred Zsa Zsa encouragingly.

"On second thought, I might replace DeBusschere with Tony's father."

See, this is an easy decision for guys. With guys, the beauty of it is, you can say to another guy, "Hey, you're a total schmuck, and I swear nobody on this island can stand you, okay?" And an hour later he'll be back, asking if you want to go to a movie or something. Whereas with a woman, you tell her that she's getting on your nerves, she goes nuts! She cries. She disappears. Worse, when she does come back she's going to want to "talk about this." What's wrong with women is they don't understand the simple elegance of solving a problem by punching somebody in the mouth.

Zsa Zsa took one last shot. She went over to Jay, a man of her generation, her attitude. She told him the deal: Five companions. No sex.

"He'll pick a woman," Zsa Zsa predicted.

Jay quickly chose Charles Barkley and Malcolm X. "We'll probably need housing," he said, so he picked Bob Vila. "We need a cook," he said. Saying "cook" instead of "chef" made me a bit nervous. But Jay came through with Paul Prudhomme. Four down, one to go.

"We gotta have a female," Jay said. "For aesthetic beauty."

Zsa Zsa, who normally would have exploded into rage at such a swinish remark, beamed.

Jay decided on Tyra Banks.

"I just want to make sure you understand that there's no sex involved," I cautioned him.

"Yeah, I know," Jay said. "But I'm picking Tyra just in case the rules change."

Next week: Same desert island—but everybody's blind!

Girls and Guise

My friend Nancy recently had minor foot surgery and afterward was advised to stay off her feet for a while. After a few days her household food supply dwindled, until one night she had only a can of soup for dinner. The next day she phoned her husband at work and, in her usual cheerful manner, mentioned there was nothing in the house to eat.

"No problem," her husband said. "I'll eat out."

This provoked one of the most common fights between men and women—the fight about women never coming out and saying what they want. (Or, if you're a woman, the fight about how men are totally insensitive louts.)

Her husband reacted like any man would, with selflessness and sympathy. He heard her say there's no food in the house. He saw she was laid up with a bad foot. He didn't want her to go to any trouble. So he said, "Honey, I'll eat out." Presumably, if there was anything left over, he would bring it home for her.

Seems reasonable to me! But I am a man. Women are not brought up to say what they want. They only hint at it. But it's stupid to hint to men. Men don't understand subtlety. That's why they read books by Tom Clancy. Men are like mules. If you want them to move forward, you have to hit them in the behind with a ball-peen hammer.

After all these years how could women not understand this?

(Women are not only too subtle, but far too demanding; for example, when you're dropping them off at a movie, so they can buy tickets while you park the car, most women actually expect you to come to a COMPLETE STOP to let them out.)

I'm sure most men feel the world would be a better place if everyone thought like a man. I always figured women believed this too. I figured women would actually like to *be* men. Amazingly, though, IT TURNS OUT THEY DON'T!

I expressed astonishment at this and suggested to my friend Tracee that there were many advantages to being a man, not the least of which was the ability to haul PVC pipe. She said, and I'm quoting here, "You're a dope, you're an idiot." Tracee also worries that her name, spelled that way, is too identifiable, so for the remainder of the column I shall call her Tracy, to protect her privacy.

Anyway, Tracy's position flabbergasts me, as I personally

can think of only one reason for a man to be a woman and that is: to play from the red tees.

On the other hand, I can think of thirty-seven obvious advantages to being a man. Here they all are:

1. You can relieve yourself more easily in the woods.

2. You can drink directly out of the carton.

3. You don't have to pretend to be offended by dirty jokes.

37. You can exaggerate shamelessly; it's macho.

Recently, Tracy, who is five feet tall, bought a twenty-seven-inch TV. The store loaded it into the trunk of her car. The box was too big and heavy for her to lift. So when she got home she faced a problem getting the set into her house.

"Why not call a man?" I asked.

"You don't call a man for a TV," she explained. "You call a man for a refrigerator."

"Well, maybe a man could help you set it up," I said.

She laughed. "Men can't figure out electronic equipment," she said. "Women can program VCRs better than men. Men can't program them at all. Men don't read the instructions. It's just like men don't ask for directions when they're driving. Men don't ponder. Men have no patience. The instruction manual that comes with an electronic device is the least read item by a man in the history of paper products."

"Oh," I said adroitly.

Anyway, to get the TV out of her car, Tracy propped two wooden boards against the fence in her driveway, backed her car to the two-by-fours—thus building a small plat-form—and without really lifting the TV, she rocked the carton onto the boards. Then she got a carpet cutter and began to cut holes in the TV carton.

"So the TV could breathe?" I asked smugly.

"No, so I could use them like handles and lift the box, you dork," she said.

Then she got a luggage cart she uses to wheel her suit-case to the airport, slid the TV carton onto the luggage cart, and rolled it from the driveway, across the backyard, to her house. She didn't have the strength or leverage to lift the carton more than eight inches. Still, she wrestled it up the steps and slid it through the house on a towel so she wouldn't scratch the floor. (Can you imagine a man think-ing to lay a towel down? A man wouldn't care about a few scratches in the floor. A man would not care about deep gouges in the floor. A man might draw the line at letting a friend drive a snowmobile into his living room, but maybe not. Tough call.) But Tracy couldn't lift the TV onto the TV stand.

"So then you called a man, right?" I asked.

"No," she said.

She built small scaffolds. She lifted the TV six inches onto a box that held a VCR. She lifted the TV six inches again, onto an ottoman. She rolled the ottoman to the TV stand and lifted the TV the final six inches to the stand.

"A man would have done it differently," I said.

And I described how a man would have picked the TV out of the trunk, by himself, danced around frantically for a second, gotten a hernia, dropped the TV on his foot, breaking the TV and the foot. Then, because men can't handle pain nearly as well as women ("Just one day I'd like to give all of you guys the cramps," Tracy said, "and once a month there wouldn't be a single man in a single office all across America"), a man would have gone home and stayed in bed for a month.

He would not run out of food.

Nancy would know to get it for him.

Upholster Boy

$\mathbf{F}$riends of mine, Peter and Julie, are decorating their house. Well, Julie is decorating. Peter is simply signing the checks.

So far the redecoration has cost him $3,300—and that's just for cushions and pillows in the family room. When Peter heard the price he asked Julie, "Who sewed the pillows, Dr. Christiaan Barnard?"

He couldn't believe he was spending $3,300 for one room. "And we're not even getting a solid gold moose head? Julie, we're doing a family room. For thirty-three hundred I can buy a whole family! How can cushions be so expensive? I can go to Pier 1 and get ten cushions for twenty-nine ninety-five each, and in a year, when I'm sick of the color, I CAN USE THEM FOR ARCHERY PRAC-

TICE THEN SET THEM ON FIRE AND STILL SAVE
THREE THOUSAND DOLLARS!"

It all kind of sneaked up on Peter. He didn't see it
coming—it was a good-cop/bad-cop kind of deal. The
owner of the studio, Louis, came to Peter's house, looked
at Peter's furniture, such as the leather beanbag chairs,
the fishnet pole lamps, the extremely attractive Chinese
lanterns stretched across the living room, the glen-plaid
sofa bed, and the neon MILLER HIGH LIFE sign, and he said,
"Yeah, we can work with this." Then he and Peter went out
on the porch, had a couple of beers, and talked about the
Redskins. And afterward Peter told Julie, "I admit I was a
little nervous hiring a decorator, but I can work with this
Lou."

The next day Lou sent his assistant, Fabulana, over to
plan the design, and the first thing she said as she walked
through the door was "Oh, God!" She stopped in her
tracks and pointed to the rug in the hallway—Peter's pride
and joy, a red-and-white thatched mohair rug with the
outline of the Zig-Zag man in royal blue, which Peter got
for twenty bucks when he was still in college—and she
said, "You're kidding . . . aren't you?"

"I want Lou back," Peter said.

But by then it was too late. Six weeks later Julie showed
Peter a few squares of cloth in colors and textures that
resembled potholders from Liberace's house and asked
Peter, "Okay, which fabric do you want?"

Now, this is a loaded question. It is a no-win for a man,

just like "Do you think I look fat in this dress?" is a no-win for a man. (No, saying "no" is not good enough. "No" implies that she *is* fat and the dress is cleverly hiding it. The only safe answer is to fake a heart attack or burst aneurysm, until the dress-opinion crisis passes.)

Anyway, with swatches of fabric, *which* one you like doesn't make any difference.

They're all unbelievably expensive.

Asking which one you like is like asking, "And how would you like those lashes across the buttocks, forehand or backhand?"

These fabrics are sold in deceptive ways.

Ah, yes, a wise choice, Crustacean Pink Twill, and a splendid bargain at two dollars and four cents per square millimeter.

Er, which comes out to . . . ?

Fifty-six thousand, four hundred and eight dollars, and that's for the toilet-seat cover.

For the most part—as long as they have one room to themselves, preferably a bathroom—men couldn't care less about decorating. A woman can totally make over a room, spend eight thousand dollars on lamps alone, bring in a handwoven rug from Jaboogoostan, and a man will look at the new room and shrug, and walk right through to the kitchen and open up the refrigerator and look for a chicken leg. The next day he won't even remember if the old room had a statue of Dag Hammarskjöld.

Men adapt to their surroundings. They're not discriminating. They don't know Scandinavian modern from

French Provincial or Italian Renaissance. If you ask men what style of furniture they prefer, nine out of ten will say, "Wood."

My friend Nancy decorated her living room in what she calls "yuppie casual." She ordered comfortable overstuffed chairs and couches and did them in chenille and tea-stained linens. It's quite beautiful. But all her husband wants is a La-Z-Boy recliner right in the middle of it. One of the big ones, with a tray table, and the magazine pouches on the side, and the vibrator and the heater, and the Velcro attachment for the TV clicker; I think you get a choice of leather or a beer-retardant fabric.

"I can't have *that* in my living room," Nancy said forlornly. "It's just hideous."

I don't understand. It's not like her husband is asking for something that doesn't go with the room, like a ski lift or a urinal. A La-Z-Boy goes with anything.

Men like big chairs. Period.

A woman goes out and blows all the dough on the tiny details in chintz and rosewood that make the room a replica of Monet's sunporch in Giverny, and a guy signs the check—and then he says, "Just gimme a big chair. So I can fall asleep watching TV."

"There's no TV in this room," the woman will say.

"Fine, then just give me a big chair where there is a TV, and if there isn't any TV there either, then give me a gun so I can shoot the decorator."

The Story Of 0

What if scientists developed an "orgasm pill" for women?

It may be in the works, according to a recent story that moved on the wires. My first reaction to the news was that this pill would be bad for men. If we men were no longer needed to dependably bring women to orgasm with our irresistible, manly ways, what need would there be for us?

"This may come as a shock to you," my friend Megan told me, "but you aren't needed for that. Fortunately for you, there are many, many bookshelves that need installing."

I assumed that women would welcome an orgasm pill. My friend Liz, who has barely any time for herself, being a working mom with two small kids, said she might take the pill while she was doing the family laundry. "And I'd have both hands free to fold," she said happily.

But Liz said that what women would rather have was a pill that would do things that men weren't good at. "Like tell you if your skirt and blouse matched, or that this is the most delicious dinner ever." Or it would confess, "My biggest flaw is that I don't listen enough to what you say, dear."

On reflection, though, I think an orgasm pill for women would be good for men. Because then, after a satisfying sexual episode that typically lasts, oh, thirty-five seconds, a man wouldn't have to waste time cuddling with a woman and pillow talking to her to convince her she was more important in his life at that moment than, say, a twelve-piece Chicken McNuggets Value Meal. He could just flip her a pill and grab the clicker and get back to the NBA game on TNT before the end of the third quarter.

To me, the most obvious question about the original orgasm pill story, the thing that should have made it suspect on its face, was: How can you reliably time it?

Let's say it takes twenty to thirty minutes to hit. So you plan it to kick in, say, toward the end of your lunch hour. But, see, let's say you ate a grilled cheese sandwich. Dairy products are murder on the digestive process. So you've had this uneventful lunch, and now you are due back for your afternoon appointment . . . testifying before the Senate Judiciary Committee on your nomination to be a United States Supreme Court justice.

And there you are on the stand, and Senator Orrin

Hatch says, "Miss Jones, we are not concerned with your politics here; that would be inappropriately partisan of us. We are concerned with questions of constitutional prerogatives, such as whether the Constitution protects unborn babies from murderous assaults by filthy subhuman godless heathens. Would you not agree, Miss Jones?"

"Yes."

"And would you also agree that even as the Constitution guarantees the separation of church and state, it encourages the freedom of religion?"

"Yes. Yessss."

"And furthermore, Miss Jones, don't you think that reinstitution of the phrase 'under God' in the Pledge of Allegiance can be construed as a return to the sacred moral and ethical values that this country was founded on?

"Oh, God, yes! Yessss! YESSSSSSS!"

"Thank you, Miss Jones. Er, there is no cigarette smoking permitted in this committee room."

GOING

MOBILE

The Buick Stops Here

This morning I went out to my car. I approached from the back, which is the vehicle's south wing, and greeted the rear navigator, the guy stationed in a little trailer cab with a steering wheel. Approaching the primary driver's quarters from the port side, I stopped twice to rest and refresh myself from a canteen I had prepared for my journey. Eventually, I gained entry through the main proscenium archway and, settling into the brocaded davenport, proceeded to initiate the ignition sequence preparatory to disembarkation of the dreadnought from my driveway.

I've bought me a new car. It is a Buick.

Yes, I, like you, have always believed Buicks were owned only by someone's fat, bald father. I still believe that. The thing is, now *I'm* someone's fat, bald father.

Buick is one of the last vestiges of the American car industry that flourished when nobody cared about gas mileage or the environment or efficient design or anything, back when the main purpose of a car was to (1) accelerate fast enough to balloon out your cheeks like those guys in the rocket sled experiments; (2) support tail fins that looked like pontoons; and (3) have a rear seat big enough to comfortably boink on. This ended with the gas crisis, when Japan and Germany began to produce peppy little cars with engines the size of Chiclets. Nowadays, all cars are small. Have you seen the new commercials for the Cadillac Sedan DeVille? Devilles used to take up two time zones. This one looks like a loaf of bread.

Through all of this downsizing, though, Buick refused to give in. Buick kept making hogs. Buick was true to the American Road. Nobody *bought* Buicks, of course, because they were monstrosities. But hey, that's the price you pay for principles. As Patrick Henry said, "Give me a Roadmaster with chrome up the yin-yang, or give me death."

So I bought a Buick.

I love it. The trunk alone could accommodate the entire machine-gunned Bonanno family.

(People in my neighborhood warned me not to buy an American car, but I think I have beaten the odds, because I have already driven it around the block more than once without the front seat falling through the floorboards, grinding me into road sausage.)

It's funny, but before I got a Buick I never noticed Buicks on the road. Now I see them everywhere. They are hard to miss; the only thing bigger on the highway are those cheesy prefab houses encased in Saran Wrap and being hauled on trailers.

Those Buicks that are not driven by obvious Mafia hit men (vanity plate: SLAY 4 U) appear to be driven by no one. That is because the driver is invisible from behind. From what I can tell by casual inspection, the average Buick owner is four feet eleven, eighty-three years old, and, basically, is one big fused liver spot.

You know the slogan "Wouldn't you really rather have a Buick?" When I picture the people actually behind the wheel of a Buick, I imagine them saying, "Compared to what, a hearse?"

I knew Buick wasn't aimed at anyone my age when I saw one of the options was handrails.

Still, I love this car. It's so, um, so . . . retro! Behind the wheel, I feel like Perry Como. I have started wearing cardigans and humming when I drive.

I was afraid my children would be embarrassed to be seen in a Buick with me. But my daughter assured me it wasn't the Buick—she's simply embarrassed to be seen with me! "It's not what you drive, Dad, it's the stupid way you sing along with the music on your boring oldies station. By the way, Dad, aren't most of the singers who were popular when you were young dead now?"

Actually, I think they're driving Buicks.

The only teensy complaint I have is that this baby gets only—this is not an underexaggeration—nine miles to the gallon.

I phoned the dealer to complain. He asked me how many miles I'd driven.

I said, "About six hundred."

He said, "Your gas mileage will improve after, uh, two thousand miles."

I think he pulled two thousand out of a hat. I think he said two thousand figuring that I am a typical Buick owner—meaning that I drive ten miles a week and that I suffer short-term memory loss. He probably figured that by the time I get to two thousand miles, I'll still be getting nine miles a gallon but I'll have forgotten the conversation.

Now I have to say that this mileage thing makes me feel a little bit piggy. I am from the generation that believed in having a social conscience, at least so long as it helped facilitate the pursuit of chicks. So I am not proud of having a gas guzzler.

This baby drinks. If every car on the road was a Buick, the tiny oil-rich kingdom of Dubai would be pumped dry in three years, and members of the Dubai royal family would have to get jobs in Nogales sweatshops making novelty toys.

Hmm.

Maybe I shouldn't feel that bad.

Auto Erratic

A woman I work with, who's about my age, is in the market for a new car. The last time she bought a car was ten years ago. At the time her children were small so she went shopping for a safe, sturdy, celibate four-door car . . . and had a midlife crisis inside the car dealership that caused her to drive off in a spiffy convertible.

I asked why she did that.

"Because," she said, shaking her shoulders like Charo doing kootchy-kootchy, "you know."

After ten years, the "you know" has been exorcised. "I just wouldn't feel comfortable buying a sports car again," she said. "And this is because, I'm, uh . . ."

An old bag? I volunteered.

"Yes, an old bag," she said. "So what does an old bag buy?"

A 1973 Nova always worked for me.

Let me caution you right away: This is not a man-woman thing. This is not about how women buy cars as opposed to men. This is not about how women are old bags. I am an old bag too.

This is a middle-age thing.

This is about finding your identity through what you drive.

Twenty years ago you bought cramped cars with low fuel consumption to do your part to help protect the environment. Ten years ago you bought bulky cars with childproof door locks so you could protect your kids. Now your kids are driving their own cars, and you couldn't care less what gas costs as long as you don't have to wait in line for it. This next car is for you—if only you knew who you were.

I am past the convertible stage now. A couple of years ago I coveted a Mazda Miata. I went to test drive it and I felt I was sitting in a shoe box; I thought about my chances of surviving an accident, and not even with another car— if my Miata got hit by a large dog, they'd have to scrape me off the road with a spatula. What clinched the deal was that when my test drive ended I couldn't get out of the car. My center of gravity was too low. I had no push-off. I had to sort of roll out onto one knee. If you're going to buy a car, at least you ought to be able to get out of it without risking arthroscopic surgery.

Auto Erratic

The same is true of jeeps and small trucks, which everybody seems to want now, as if paved roads were going out of style. Am I missing something here? Are we preparing to occupy Switzerland, and this is the way we're crossing the Alps? Does anybody really need a Range Rover in Washington? For what, for those terrible mudslides on the Beltway? Riding in a jeep is like riding in a tin can—even the chic Eddie Bauer Limited Edition. Half the time you feel like you're in a Cuisinart and somebody hit the "pulse" button. And you're sitting so high you can get vertigo. A friend of mine shelled out $27,000 for a Chevy Blazer, and asked for the stepladder option so he could drive it home. I'll bet the highest incidence of broken legs among middle-aged men is caused by dismounting from Ford Broncos.

Getting back to my friend: She stares at cars all the time now, trying to figure out which one is *her.* She goes to the supermarket but doesn't actually buy food—which hasn't endeared her at home—because she spends all her time walking through the parking lot casing cars. (She told me that one of her friends suggested she forget about the Giant, and go upscale and cruise the lot at Sutton Place Gourmet. "But I never shop there," my friend said. I gently pointed out to her that she never *shops* anywhere anymore; she is the automotive equivalent of a Bedouin nomad chasing the perfect date-palm oasis.) Recently she was out jogging and spotted a car she liked stopped at a light. She yelled out to the driver, "What've you got under the hood?" The terrified man—obviously thinking that a woman in jogging shorts who approached his car to ask him a question like that must be a prostitute—quickly shut his window and sped away.

"It was an Altima," she remembered. "Who makes Altima?"

Who makes Altima? Who makes Avalon? Who makes Millenia? Cirrus? Aurora? They all look like fat Fabergé eggs. Are they Japanese? Are they American? (Hint: They're not European, because European cars don't have names, just letters and numbers. C-280; 300SEL; 525i. Anybody out there got Bingo?)

Remember when it was simpler, when cars had rules? You were a Ford man or a GM man. If you were a GM man, you started with a Chevy, you bought an Olds when you got married, and if you got a promotion—whoa, here comes Mr. Buick! You moved up within the known order. The kind of car you owned reflected your spot in the food chain.

Now it's so confusing. Nobody's a Ford man anymore, nobody sticks with a company his whole life; if Henry Ford were alive today, he'd probably drive a Lexus! Madison Avenue has made us a nation of car-buying Sybils. How can your car tell you who you are when every year three hundred new cars come out, each one promising a sleeker, safer, more roomy you? Whatever happened to Plymouth Furys, which didn't promise you anything but a radio and a heater?

American manufacturers are afraid to put an American

nameplate on the car, because if you know it's an American car, you'll assume after you drive five blocks the engine will explode, and you'll have to be towed—usually by a Toyota. They want you to think it's Japanese. If the folks who made Aurora were any more closemouthed about it being an Oldsmobile, Marcel Marceau would be in the passenger seat.

On the other hand, Japanese manufacturers are aware you want to do the patriotic thing, so they stress their cars are "assembled in the United States"—like this makes you think their profits aren't going straight to the Tojo War College. New cars, like Millenia and Infiniti, downplay being Japanese, because they're aiming at Americans who buy luxury European imports like BMW. Infiniti uses a British actor as a pitchman and has Euro-sounding models like J30; they'll probably give you a rebate in deutsch marks.

I feel sorry for my friend, trying to discover which car is *her.*

You can't find yourself in the vanity mirror anymore.

Stalling for Time

This is the story of my smart friend Martha, my evil editor, Gene, and the car of Gene's teenage dreams, a VW Beetle.

It is the story of why you can't go home again.

Unless you are towed.

Martha, who is originally from California, bought the Beetle in 1988, when it already had 76,000 miles. "All the cute girls back home drive that car, and I was trying to be cute again," she explained. Over the next two years she put four thousand dollars and 5,500 miles into it. She also painted it black, "so that when I got out in a cocktail dress, I wouldn't look stupid."

The car ran great, except for when it broke down and had to be towed: ten times in a little more than two years.

One day Martha got into her Beetle to drive to work,

and it wouldn't start. She had a pretty good parking spot, so she left it sitting there for *two months*. When Martha returned, the car had been booted. It now not only needed repair and a tow, it needed bail, the sum of which vastly outweighed cute.

Enter Gene, salivating.

"I always wanted a VW Bug. I thought it would connect me to all those wild, impetuous feelings I had when I was seventeen," explained Gene, who was seventeen as recently as 1969.

Martha offered to sell Gene the car. Well, not sell it, exactly. She'd give it to him if he paid all the costs, which amounted to $401.19.

"A steal," she said.

"A steal," he agreed.

Martha straightforwardly warned Gene about the car's recent ailments. His only reluctance concerned the hole in the floorboard, which was so invitingly large you could pass a football through it. "Not one of those things your kid gets at Hardee's, either," Gene said. "NFL regulation size." Gene feared he "would drop through this hole while still in my seat and be decapitated as the car rolled over my head."

Looking for assurance, Gene consulted America's best-loved feature writer, Mr. Henry, who had owned three VW Bugs himself—one of which sputtered to a stop in New York, one of which blew up in Colorado after approximating "the sound of a berserk threshing machine attempting to kill itself," and one of which Mr. Henry last saw gushing oil in New Mexico. "My favorite was the one I had in college," he recalled. "The problem was, it didn't have windshield-wiper fluid, so in the winter months I'd suck right up behind big trucks, hoping they'd splash a load of slush on me." But of course, that's another story.

Mr. Henry assured Gene that Martha's Beetle was indeed a steal.

"What about the hole?" Gene asked.

"They all have holes," Mr. Henry said.

"So I won't be decapitated after I fall through?"

"No. More likely, you'll be pitched forward onto your face, which will be ground against the highway like a felt-tip pen made out of meat."

Armed with all this, what did Gene do?

He bought the car.

"My life," Gene concluded, "would be incomplete otherwise."

(What is it with VW Beetles? How come everyone over forty either owned one or has a story to tell? "Some of the best days and nights of my life were spent in a VW Bug," my friend Nancy recalled. "Like that time we went to see the Who and ended up in a ditch and . . . oh, Tony, no, you can't tell that story. I have a son!" I myself remember driving cross-country in a blue '64 Bug. There were three college students and all our luggage—one change of underwear and a jug of Boone's Farm wine; the '60s, you know. I couldn't even get my thigh in that car now.)

Anyway, Gene bought it as is, without a heater, with the

hole, with a radio that only holds the station for a quarter-mile unless you keep one hand on the tuner ("which complicates shifting"), a solitary can of cat food in the glove compartment that Martha identified as "emergency rations," and—perhaps Gene should have taken this as a bad sign—a set of highway flares in the backseat.

Joyously, Gene drove his new prize out of the parking lot where Martha left it for him, and he got *ten full blocks* before it broke down and had to be towed.

This came as no surprise to Martha, who recalled that the very first time she drove it, it broke down too. "It's like a good woman," she said. "It won't let you get it home the first night. . . . Did I tell you I bought it from a drug dealer?" But of course, that too is another story.

The second time he drove the car, Gene got all the way to his kids' school. And back! Slightly more than one mile. "She purred like a kitten."

The third time Gene was cruising like James Dean, going nearly forty for more than two miles, when the accelerator cable snapped. Suddenly, he decelerated to three miles an hour, the actual, terrifyingly vulnerable, unable-to-get-to-the-side-of-the-road speed a vehicle travels when its engine is disconnected from the driver's foot, on Wisconsin Avenue, at midday, in whizzing traffic. The car had to be towed.

Having heard this story, I asked Mr. Henry why he advised Gene to buy such a pooch of a car.

Mr. Henry contemplated the question for quite a while, then said, "Now that I think of it, I was wrong."

Nonetheless, Gene feels reborn and remains dopey with delight over his Beetle:

"This is the finest car I have ever owned."

"Of course he loves the car," says Martha. "I loved that car too. My one regret is that I never took a picture of it." (If you see Martha, you might tell her the car is currently available for a photo opportunity, on the back of a tow truck at Connecticut and Nebraska.)

Gene is determined to keep the car, whatever the cost. "It seems to me I have two choices: put my feet through the hole and drive it like Fred Flintstone, or buy a tow truck and tow it wherever I go."

"I think he looks younger," Martha observed.

The Crushing End to a
Love Affair with a Car

According to the most
recent survey, teenage girls are having more sex, and
having it earlier than ever. This is fabulous news for
teenage boys, but not as good for middle-age fathers.
I'm fortunate in that my daughter is turning eight, so sex
is not yet an issue with her. (Currently, her big issue is,
Why can't she eat apple crumb cake in the den?) But I
figured that when the time came to talk to her about sex,
I'd tell her to have it in a Volvo, because they're the safest
cars.

That's why we bought a Volvo: safety. My wife saw the ad
where seven trucks are stacked on top of a Volvo, *no prob-
lema.*

"That's the car I want," she said.

"Why?" I asked. "Are you planning on joining a truck circus?"

We bought a Volvo in 1985, and we've felt safe ever since. Should nuclear war break out, our contingency plan is to live in our Volvo, listening to ABBA tapes until the all-clear signal.

Do you know that Volvos are so safe that we're not handing out gas masks to our soldiers in Saudi Arabia anymore, we're locking them in Volvos instead?

So imagine my shock earlier in the week when Volvo admitted its ad agency had phonied up a commercial about how safe the car is. The ad shows one of those Monster Trucks—the kind with the twenty-nine-foot-high bear-claw tires driven by guys who look like they just got off the set of *Ernest Goes to Camp*—rolling over the top of a bunch of cars, crushing all the roofs except one. The underline asks: "Can you spot the Volvo?"

Obviously, the one with the roof. The others don't have enough headroom for Alfredo Garcia.

But the truth is, the Volvo was specially prepared for the filming. They reinforced its roof with lumber and steel to withstand the pounding. Volvo was ratted out to the Texas attorney general by some of the folks they'd paid to be extras where the commercial was shot in Austin. Volvo took out huge ads in some newspapers this week, explaining. The other day in Philadelphia, just for a laugh, three thirteen-thousand pound Monster Trucks re-created the ad with some standard-issue Volvos. The Volvos were, indeed, stouter than other cars on the line, so it took a few passes. Ultimately, however, the Monsters squished those Swedish babies like wine grapes.

Volvo. A Car You Can Believe In (Sometimes).

Who's their next hire, Joe Isuzu?

This is causing depression in my neighborhood, where everyone has a Volvo; Ingmar Bergman uses our block for location shots. Each of these Upper Northwest Volvos has at least 146,000 miles. Other neighborhoods, men hand women that line about coming over to see their etchings. This neighborhood, he offers to show her his odometer. Every Volvo built after 1945 is still on the street—my street.

Each weekday I see the tank brigade of Volvo station wagons (how's this for a multiple oxymoron: Volvo turbo wagon) driving by on the way to school, Mom in the front, backseats crammed with battalions of kids belted into state-of-the-art super-padded safety seats. (You know, that's the dirty little secret about Volvos: Men don't actually drive them, particularly the station wagons. Men buy them for their wives—out of concern their family might be crushed if, say, three or six trucks, parachuting wildly like Skylab, landed smack on the Mercedes—and only drive them on family outings. Men don't care about *staying* alive in a car, they care about *feeling* alive in a car. I drive a Chevette. You've heard that a Cressida is a poor man's BMW? Well, a Chevette is a homeless man's Dodge Dart. It's like going over Niagara Falls in a barrel. Even at fifteen miles an hour I'm on two wheels. My wife won't ride in the Chevette. She's even terrified when I *wash* it. When she hears it coming, she herds the kids into the Volvo.) Volvo is the only car to come with six child seats and the Aprica guide to ballet and soccer camps as standard equipment; the wagon, instead of a trunk, comes with a nursery back there. A single woman I know tried to buy a Volvo last year and the dealer wouldn't sell it to her without a signed statement attesting to her intention of bearing children within three years or 146,000 miles.

America's best-loved feature writer, Mr. Henry (ahem, a domestic-van man himself), insists that "Volvo owners are the ultimate middle-class *shlumpfs*. They come home at night, and they microwave their individual Lean Cuisine dinner and then don't talk to each other because they're too busy reading catalogs. They are people whose garbage cans are full with beautifully carved chicken skin that they don't eat. If Puritans were assigned GS ratings, they'd have all driven Volvos."

But undeniably, safety is the bogeyman of car owning these days. Have you seen that commercial where the Shell Answer Man warns women who park their car in what appears to be downtown Beirut to carry a flashlight because someone may be hiding under her car? Who hides *under* a car? You hide under a car, if you don't make your move fast enough, you're eating a tread sandwich, babe. And if you're the woman walking to your car—lady, really, couldn't you have sprung for the extra few bucks and done the valet parking?—wouldn't it be smarter to just get in and gun the engine, rather than kneel down and look under the car so this painfully thin deviate can reach out and grab you? Anyway, it turns out there is something hiding under the car. It's A CAT! So for any of you in this position, by all means carry a flashlight, and a can of 9 Lives tuna. Me? I'm buying a Monster Truck. See you on the Beltway, sucker.

RICH, FAMOUS PEOPLE WHO DON'T KNOW I EXIST

Dirty Rodman Scoundrel

The big news in publishing is that the No. 1–selling book in America this week is *Bad as I Wanna Be,* by the noted man of letters Mr. Dennis Rodman of the Chicago Bulls.

How bad does Mr. Rodman wanna be? Apparently, he wans ta be the worst writer on earth.

Have you *seen* this book?

Rodman is on the cover with his flame-broiled orange hair and his body pierced in so many places that when he drinks a liter of water he is his own sprinkler system. He is stark naked except for a strategically placed basketball. He is sitting on a huge motorcycle. His body is full of tattoos, the most prominent of which, on his left triceps, appears to be of a toilet seat.

But you cannot, hahaha, judge a book by its cover. No,

to understand the complexity of Mr. Rodman's oeuvre, it is necessary to turn to any random page, where you learn that the book's main feature is that every so often a few provocative words will suddenly BE PRINTED IN GIGANTIC SWIRLING TYPE. It is as though Mr. Rodman believes the average reader has the attention span of, you know, to use a ridiculous example, some six-foot-eight jock whose specialty in life is garnering rebounds by smashing people in the face with his elbows.

But the amazing thing is how manipulative and misleading these giant-type phrases are. Here is a quote from page 167: "I'm not gay. I would tell you if I was. If I go to a gay bar that does not mean I want ANOTHER MAN TO PUT HIS TONGUE DOWN MY THROAT. No, it means I want to be a whole individual."

Get the concept?

Hey, I can do that:

"So the other day I went to the store to get some milk and eggs, and all of a sudden I had a GUN IN MY LAP. It was my son's toy gun that he'd left in my car the night before, AND I HAD THE URGE TO PUT THE GUN TO MY HEAD AND PULL THE TRIGGER, BRO, realizing nothing would happen. All the people who might want to see

MY BRAINS SPLATTERED ALL OVER THE FRONT SEAT would have to wait for another day. Perhaps when I needed orange juice."

And then maybe I, too, will have the No. 1–selling book in the land. But I am not bitter.

Prior to his phenomenal literary success, Rodman's previous claim to fame was HE HAD SEX WITH THAT SLUT MADONNA, a best-selling author herself. Wow. It's as if Dorothy Parker had an affair with James Thurber—except for the small detail that they had brains.

If you're David Halberstam or Tom Wolfe, if you're anybody who writes ACTUAL NONFICTION BOOKS—books where the main disclosure about Madonna (page 197) isn't "SHE WASN'T AN ACROBAT BUT SHE WASN'T A DEAD FISH, EITHER," and the essential philosophical statement isn't "IF I WANT TO WEAR A DRESS, I'LL WEAR A DRESS" (page 167)— if you are Halberstam or Wolfe when you check the bestseller list and see *Bad As I Wanna Be*, you have to want to remove your eyes with a melon-ball scooper.

As Dennis Rodman has found out, the quickest way up in literature is to bounce on the pogo stick of celebrity. A good way to do that is to paint your hair orange. But the best way to do that is to get your own sitcom. In the past year Fran Drescher, Ellen DeGeneres, Paul Reiser, Brett Butler, and Tim Allen have all had best-sellers—and if they actually wrote them, I'm Jerry Mahoney. (We know Rodman didn't write his book; most people don't think he *read* it.) Isn't it strange how that works out: YOU STICK YOUR HAND IN A WALL SOCKET and grunt like a woodchuck on television— ALL OF A SUDDEN YOU'RE ERNEST HEMINGWAY! How come it doesn't work the other way? How come nobody ever asked James M. Schlesinger, Jr., to star in *The Nanny*?

You don't have to be a celebrity to write a best-seller. You could write a diet book. (Though it helps to be a celebrity *and* write a diet book, like Joan Lunden, WHO HAS STAYED ON TV FOR MORE THAN A DECADE WITH NO DISCERNIBLE TALENT. You could also write a cartoon book and get on the best-seller list, like the one about Dilbert, the office dweeb who never gets any, or the *Waldo's in Gondwanaland* books, which aren't books at all, but drawings—which is like giving the PULITZER PRIZE FOR LITERATURE TO TINKY "DAKOTA" WEISBLAT.

But all things considered, celebrity is the way to go. Personally, I'm waiting for the CHARLIE SHEEN TELL-ALL BOOK. Sheen is my idea of what a celebrity should be in the '90s—a giant, gaping keister in human clothing.

You remember that he came into prominence with the revelation that he had spent more than $53,000 on **HEIDI FLEISS'S PROSTITUTES** in a two-year period. That was followed shortly by the news that Charlie-boy was getting married! "She's an angel sent from Heaven to take me through the rest of my journey," Charlie said, revoltingly.

The journey lasted five months. "You buy a car, it breaks down, what are you gonna do?" that crazy sentimentalist Charlie said in announcing his divorce.

His sudden ex-wife claimed she was shocked, **SHOCKED TO FIND OUT CHARLIE PAID FOR ALL THOSE HOOKERS!** She said she didn't know. Huh? Everybody knew. **MY DOG KNEW.**

(The joke about the marriage was that it got off to a terrible start after the first night of the honeymoon, when Charlie asked his wife if he could start a tab.)

From there Charlie took up baseball. Not content with paying for sex, he wanted to pay for a major-league home run. So one day **HE SPENT FIVE THOU-SAND DOLLARS TO BUY ALL THE SEATS BEHIND THE LEFT-FIELD FENCE IN ANAHEIM STADIUM** so he could get a home-run ball. "I didn't want to crawl over the paying public," Charlie said. "I wanted to avoid the violence." I'm pleased to say the game that night between the Angels and Tigers was the only game all year in which there were no homers hit, and Charlie was out five large—about the same as two Heidi-ho's would have cost.

This past week Charlie resurfaced, like a fish head, claiming HE IS BORN AGAIN! He said his faith was "so far beyond me. It's so much more powerful than anything I can control. I HAVE TO SURRENDER."

Sounds like a title to me.

The Ballad of Tonya and Nancy

It's Nancy and Tonya, yes Tonya and Nancy,
Who've captured America's soap opera fancy.

Nancy's the one who succeeds in this tale,
While Tonya's the one who might go to jail.
And then she won't skate out at the mall,
Where the Clackamas K mart is just down the hall,
And eventually if Tonya should come all a cropper
We'll know when we hear: "Attention K mart shoppers."

Who'll do her makeup, who'll work on her grammar
If she's doing a stretch in the Oregon slammer?
Gillooly is going, and Eckhardt, fat foof,
Can you imagine them all underneath the same roof?
I'm sure they'll eventually feel some contrition
We'll be able to see it on *Inside Edition.*

2 1 7

RICH, FAMOUS PEOPLE WHO DON'T KNOW I EXIST

It'll take quite some time for them all to be sprung
On visiting days I expect Connie Chung
To interview Tonya and keep us informed
Of the programs she's planning, the short and the long.
And maybe, just *maybe,* I'm now theorizin',
In Nagano she'll skate in the pairs with Mike Tyson.

It's Nancy and Tonya, yes Tonya and Nancy,
Who've captured America's soap opera fancy.

Now turning attention to Kerrigan's knee
Which got whacked pretty good in the Motor Ci-ty.
Her comeback was golden, most of us reckoned.
It's a shame she got nosed out and only took second.
She skated with elegance, poise, and real grace,
She was programmed to show us that smile on her face.
At no time did Nancy resemble a fool,
But she got outperformed by that waif, Ms. Baiul,
Who was perky and campy and flirty and sold
Herself to the crowd—and just sixteen years old!
Can you imagine who'll portray Oksana on screen?
Not her, she's too young, but the thought is serene
That the Hollywood moguls would go for a face,
More mature, a bit worldly, with a hint of a trace
Of the pain that a young girl can have—the eyes darting
Oh, sure, as Baiul, I can see Tonya Harding!

It's Nancy and Tonya, yes Tonya and Nancy,
Who've captured America's soap opera fancy.

2 1 8

The Ballad of Tonya and Nancy

The two hardly talked in their two weeks in Norway.
Mostly they said, "I'll go mine, you'll go your way."
But the first time they saw each other in Hamar
Not a word was exchanged regarding the slammer.
She walked over to Tonya and told her, "Hello,"
Then offered, "It's been quite a month," don't you know?
And that's about it, according to scriptures.
One last thing, Nancy added, "See you at pictures."
In the U.S. team photo where both smiled like friends,
They're strategically placed at opposite ends.
They never were put in a *mano-a-mano*
In between were Scott Davis and Brian Boitano.

They practiced together, the luck of the draw.
We wondered if they would go hammer and claw.
So we trekked to the rink, got jammed in like sardines,
All of us questioning what all of it means
To be chasing a story that had as its target
Casual readers at the supermarket
Standing on line to check out what they've bought
Perusing if Nancy and Tonya had fought.

It's Nancy and Tonya, yes Tonya and Nancy,
Who've captured America's soap opera fancy.

They waited two weeks to get into the game.
Through it all Nancy never mentioned the name
Of her rival. Not a "Tonya" fell from her lips.

RICH, FAMOUS PEOPLE WHO DON'T KNOW I EXIST

If you said it, she'd stand there, her hands on her hips
And a scowl on her face as she tossed back her hair
Which, when out of that bun, well, it hangs down to there.
And those teeth, Nancy surely has more teeth than most,
They're so large and so white, they're as white as a ghost.
She wears white on the ice, white suits her the best.
Tonya rarely wears white, except for the dress
That she wore to her wedding, the dress she unzipped
When Jeff focused the camera and said, "Let 'er rip."

Nancy's lovely and really quite bursting with charms.
Whereas Tonya—what's the deal with those underarms?
The night of the final Tonya's life came unglued.
She was panicked and crying, and then she was booed
By the people who'd seen Tonya over and over
Pop a dress, break a lace, and request a do-over.
Tonya has played them so often for fools
That Nancy said angrily, "They're bending the rules."
But she shrugged as if it's just par for the course
That everyone here would just scream themselves hoarse.

And Tonya would still do it all her own way
Which explains why the feelings we're feeling today
Is one skater beloved—on the other we're hazy;
We're afraid that she might, well, she could just go crazy.
And here Nancy sits with her offers aplenty
She sells Campbell's and cameras and pasta al dente.
While Tonya is knee-deep in lawyers and threats.

2 2 0

The Ballad of Tonya and Nancy

"Knee-deep," that's irony, or couldn't you guess?

Yes, Nancy and Tonya, Tonya and Nancy,
Who've captured America's soap opera fancy.
And kept us intrigued and involved and enraged.
What a shame that they're finally leaving the stage.

Hugh Making Me Crazy

Can't somebody please make Hugh Grant shut up and go away?

Hugh Grant has been on TV more than O.J. He's been on Leno, Larry King, the *Today* show, Regis and Kathie Lee, and he's booked for Letterman. If you missed all of those, you can catch him on *Good Morning, Cedar Rapids* and the Cruising Channel.

Every time I look up, he's apologizing again. Stop being such a sissy boy.

Nobody has said "I'm sorry" this much since Brenda Lee.

"I'm sorry. I'm despicable. I don't know what got into me. It was madness. I've disgraced myself, disgraced my girlfriend, disgraced all of England, and the queen

222

(though I got a nice note of encouragement from Prince Charles). I'm so ashamed. Please forgive me."

Wink-wink.

He comes out sheepishly with his head bowed, his hair artificially tousled, his shirt wrinkled from torment. He sits down, shifting his weight uncomfortably in his seat. He blinks his eyes a lot, almost becoming teary. He says that it was really awful what he did, really awful, disgusting actually, repulsive, *yeecchhh!*

Then they go to break, and when they come back Grant blithely talks up his new movie, which, by virtue of Grant being caught in the backseat of a BMW with his pants hanging out the window, is a runaway box-office bonanza. And when Grant is done, everyone applauds like crazy. Men applaud because they find what Grant did—stepping out on a bodacious babe like Elizabeth Hurley—so darned encouraging. Women applaud because when Grant crinkles up his forehead and says, "Well, ah, of course, one is terribly, terribly embarrassed by these shenanigans," he's just so cute. The little pisher now has millions of women who'd jump in the backseat with him for free! Any day now there will be bumper stickers that say, I'LL DO HUGH.

Great career move, I'd say.

The other night Larry King called Hugh Grant "the next Cary Grant." A few months ago Hugh Grant wasn't even the next *Lou* Grant.

So stop with this pasty fake-wimp act, where you insincerely confess your loathsomeness, and because you do it in an Oxford accent everyone swoons and thinks you should be knighted.

Big stars don't act like that. You think Robert De Niro would apologize if he were caught with a hooker on Sunset Boulevard? No way. De Niro hasn't apologized for *Stanley and Iris.* John Wayne? The Duke was so honorable, he'd have *married* her. You think Marlon Brando would have gotten himself in this pickle? Are you kidding me? Brando couldn't *fit* in the backseat of a BMW. The problem is that male movie stars have changed. In his *Hang 'Em High* days, Clint Eastwood would have spit through his teeth and shot everyone on Sunset with one bullet. But Eastwood went soft in *The Bridges of Madison County* and now they all are . . . well, maybe soft is an inappropriate word in this case.

At least Grant hasn't blamed his inner child for this. Maybe he's not completely in touch with his feelings yet— though that could be because someone else in that BMW was in touch with Hugh's feelings.

(And why is Elizabeth Hurley so upset with him? She always has that "Who passed gas?" look when she's with him. Given what we know about Brit sex scandals, she should be happy. At least Grant was wearing men's under- wear, and the hooker was a woman.)

Katie Couric asked Grant about his sentencing, and Grant actually said, "I've always been willing to pay the same price as the next man." But Man About Town Chip Muldoon contradicts that: "Hugh Grant's mistake was not being cash-liquid. He got horny in Hollywood. We all do. But he only had sixty dollars, so he had to do it in a car instead of a hotel. That's why most of us have the good sense to never carry less than a hundred dollars."

There's only one solution. After a week of this interminable confessing, I want something like the V-chip that President Clinton says will zap off your TV set when a violent program comes on. I want a T-chip, a Tony chip, that will get rid of everyone who annoys me.

Imagine, here comes another Susan Powter infomercial. *Zap!* Greta Van Susteren babbling about O.J., Richard Simmons just babbling. *Zap! Zap!*

And I'm just getting started.

Alan Dershowitz, shut up and get out now. Go to the airport. Leave.

Roseanne Barr-Arnold-Fortensky-Rodham-Clinton, Johnnie Cochran, Lance Ito, I'm begging you, just go.

Bruce Willis, Demi Moore, Richard Gere, Cindy Crawford (I mean, could we at least *consider* the possibility of having a magazine cover without them?).

Michael Eisner, it's the mouse, not you, stupid. Barbra Streisand. (Yes, it's easy to list her but necessary.) Bill Gates, Boris Yeltsin, the Infiniti guy, anyone connected with *Dateline NBC*, Ken Burns, Siskel . . . or is it Ebert? Scott O'Grady, time's up, thank you. Jim Carrey, it's one move, and we've seen it. *Zap* all of them.

Dick Cavett. It's over. Deal with it! You too, Bill Moyers. And Rolonda, I'm so sick of you and Jenny Jones pretending to be shocked by your guests. If you don't want Lesbian Dwarf Skinheads Who Sleep with Their Lovers' Fathers, don't book them. Now get out.

Courtney Love. Give her a doggie bag, call her a cab.

Michael Jackson, Bob Packwood, Al Sharpton, Joey Buttafuoco, check, please.

The bus is loading. Be on it.

Test Your TV Sleaze IQ

These are hard times in America. We no longer manufacture the best cars or the best clothes or the best electronic products. The only things we seem good at producing are talk-show guests. These, thanks to the miracle of television, we have in endless supply. Loons of a feather flocking together.

Daily, we are treated to amazing performances. On one particular show—it was the unconscionably unctuous Sally Jessy Raphaël, but it doesn't really matter because all the talk shows would book this act in a heartbeat— sat a couple of transsexual men who had become lesbians. Think of this now: men who were miserably unhappy being men, men who felt themselves to be women trapped in men's bodies, men who presumably wanted to become women because they felt discomfort at being sexually attracted to other men. They went through the physical and emotional torment of surgery, *and then became lesbians*! Talk about taking the long way home.

These shows have become an absurd parody of themselves.

What do you mean, Tony?

This is what I mean: Of the thirty-five items listed below, eleven actually were recent talk-show topics. The rest I made up. See if you can guess which are real. Answers will be provided.

1. Nuns who are secretly men.
2. Dogs who can play ticktacktoe.
3. Siamese twins who are in a pickle: One wants to be a housewife, and the other wants to be a doctor.
4. Four vampires from Ohio.
5. Parents whose children mistakenly ate cherry and peach pits and needed surgery when live plants began growing in their intestines.
6. A Wisconsin man who invented a car powered by bees.
7. Admitted necrophiliacs—and the women who loved them.
8. Julio Iglesias's dentist.
9. Little, skinny men who like big, fat women.
10. The Girls of the KKK.
11. A woman who claims to be an alien from the second moon of Neptune, and her stepbrother, Andrew.
12. Neighbors of convicted serial killers.

13. Middle-aged men who have been traumatized by their inability to grow whiskers.

14. A West Virginia woman who weaves quilts out of nasal hairs.

15. Eight sadomasochists seeking to establish a political action committee.

16. A geneticist who has bred a wild moose down to the size of a desktop stapler.

17. Six bald men who have tattooed their heads so that when they stand together and bend over, their scalps form a perfect scale model of Picasso's *Guernica*.

18. Sons and daughters of hookers and pimps.

19. A woman who is being sued by her condominium association for raising bats.

20. Six Mexican trampolinists born without feet.

21. Three completely naked couples—one gay, one lesbian, and one heterosexual—who fondle each other onstage at an art museum.

22. People who have married animals.

23. An elected official who fell from power after being videotaped smoking crack cocaine in a hotel room, who says his real problem is that he is a "sex addict."

24. Gay men who got married on camera as the studio audience threw rice.

25. Transvestite California highway patrolmen who are suing for the right to wear sundresses while riding their police motorcycles.

26. People who are too fat to walk and are demanding the use of publicly funded forklifts.

27. People who haven't had a bowel movement in a year.

28. Mothers and daughters who share their men.

29. Neighbors of children who have been raised by wolves.

30. Women who have fallen in love with the men who raped them.

31. Tap-dancing albinos.

32. Men who have married their grandmothers.

33. Men who have married their daughters.

34. A California teenager who got a breast transplant from her mother.

35. Everyone who has ever known Michele Cassone.

Answers below:

11 correct: You call this living?

6–10 correct: You watch too much crap TV.

3–5 correct: You were guessing better.

How to score: 0–3 correct: You were guessing.

33, and 35.

The real items are Nos. 3, 9, 10, 18, 21, 23, 24, 28, 30,

Billy Martin's
Own Kind of Game

My mother tried to teach me that if I didn't have anything nice to say about somebody, I shouldn't say anything at all.

Sorry, Mom.

Billy Martin always brought out the worst in me. He still does. Whenever I think of him, I remember sportswriter John Schulian's description of Billy: "a mouse studying to become a rat."

I used to write about that beer commercial in which he cutely protested, "I didn't punch no doggie." I wrote, "No, Billy shot the doggie."

Some will remember him as a great baseball manager, and for a while he was. Wherever he went his teams did better the first year under him than they had in a long time, phenomenally better sometimes; it was like a magic booster shot. It was only after Billy left that folks began to comb through the litter of overworked pitching arms and broken spirits he left behind. "Billyball" was grounded in the belief that enemies were necessary for success. Billy would first turn the players against the press, then he'd turn them against the owner or some other authority figure who he'd insist was bent on destroying him, then he'd turn most of the players against some of the players; ask Reggie Jackson about it. Billy felt you couldn't win unless you had someone to hate. Every one of his locker rooms was redolent with the nervous scent of fear and loathing. Unfortunately, Billy wasn't simply self-destructive.

He won five division titles, two pennants, and one World Series. You'd think teams would want to hold on to a manager that good. But Billy never stayed long. There'd be a fistfight—either with an opposing player or one of his own players or a team official or a marshmallow salesman or some patrons at the Copacabana in New York or three unnamed assailants at a urinal in a topless bar in Texas; as Billy's idol and father figure, Casey Stengel, liked to say, "You could look it up"—and Billy would be gone. Billy couldn't stay away from fights. Or bars. Jim Hegan, a man who was a major-league catcher for seventeen years, and later a coach on the Yankees, a man who knew Billy Martin for a long time, told me ten years ago, "One day you'll pick up the paper and read that Billy was killed in a bar fight."

All those words that have come to stand for something admirable in today's America—"scrappy," "feisty," "combative," "unyielding"—Billy was all of those. Between the white lines they produced an overachieving player and a successful manager. But Billy was given to great excess. He drank too much and fought too much. He was quick-tempered and nasty. If you weren't all the way with him, you were his enemy, and he never reconciled with an enemy.

In 1988, when he was honored by the Yankees by having his number retired—an honor bestowed on the likes of Ruth, DiMaggio, Gehrig, and Mantle—Billy was asked if there was any one thing he'd change in his life, after all the fights and controversies, any *one* thing? And Billy said yes, there was one, and he named a certain sportswriter and said he'd kick his tail. That's Billy Martin's view of the world: Get in the first punch. He was good at battling. He was no good at stopping, no good at leaving his battles at the ballpark. He took his demons with him. It didn't surprise anyone who knew him that he died violently. It surprised some that he lasted until sixty-one. (When I heard he'd been in a car accident, my first thought was, "Was he drunk?" The question is moot. Billy wasn't driving. His friend was. Police say his friend was drunk.)

The first time I encountered Billy, he was managing the Detroit Tigers. I'd been sent to cover a meaningless July game against the Yankees. In it there was a rare play: A runner scored all the way from second base on a wild pitch.

After the game about twenty-five reporters gathered in Billy's office. I waited for one of the more veteran scribes to ask about the wild pitch. When none did, I offered, "Pretty unusual play, huh?"

Billy glared at me. "Where'd you learn your baseball, Woolworth's?"

I was new on the block, unsure of how to respond. I grinned, thinking he was joking. "I mean you don't see a play like that often," I said meekly.

Out of nowhere Billy exploded. "That's the dumbest [expletive] question I ever heard. Who let you in here? Any you other [expletive] want to ask something that [expletive] stupid?" Seething, Billy flapped his arms to clear the room. Gesturing at me, he announced, "I'm not talking until that [expletive] leaves."

Later I asked another writer why Billy did that.

"That's Billy," I was told. "Who knows what sets him off?"

In the last ten years Billy had become a running joke thanks to the cynical efforts of George Steinbrenner, who fed Billy's neuroses by hiring, firing, rehiring, and refiring him as a convenient way to sell tickets. George and Billy were vaudevillians sharing a cow costume doing a preposterous mating dance.

A transparent manipulator like Steinbrenner may have been the only one out there who could've made Billy seem noble. Indeed, baseball fans in general and Yankee fans in particular loved Billy. Amazing, isn't it, this man will never get a sniff of the Hall of Fame, yet you can't talk about baseball in the last twenty years without mentioning his name. It didn't matter how gaunt or ravaged he looked, or how regularly he repeated the same mistakes and blamed everyone else for his failures, fans adored him. Somehow, although it wasn't true—when others willingly gave autographs at spring training, Billy would sneak out a back exit and avoid the fans altogether—they saw him as a man of the people, an underdog fighting the righteous fight, a vigilante. Even though he punched first, he was never the aggressor in their eyes, always the victim.

At his funeral, he was described as a rebel and an individualist, a man who took the blows and did it his way, an original, an American hero. They spoke of the private, caring Billy Martin, and they mentioned he was a man of God, who wore crosses on the crown of his Yankee cap. For nearly twenty years I sat in dugouts and hung around batting cages and clubhouses near him. I was in big and small rooms with him. I saw the crosses, but I never saw the kindness and charity that befit them. When I looked into his eyes, all I ever saw was anger.

Party Time in Beverly Hills

Having wanted to go to a fancy Hollywood party all my life, I was thrilled to finagle an invitation to this one—though it wasn't technically a party, but a fund-raiser to save the Amazon rain forest. Springsteen, Sting, and Billy Crystal had agreed to perform. I'd have flown to Brazil and lain in front of a bulldozer to see it; it's a once-in-a-lifetimer. Most of the parties I'm at don't have big-name entertainment, unless you count Jonathan Myron Pitagorsky donning a grass skirt and dancing the cool jerk.

"How many people are coming?" I asked the PR man.

"About eight hundred."

"And it's in someone's *backyard*?"

"It's a big backyard."

"Probably helps on a resale: 'Spacious yard, seats eight hundred comfortably.'"

The house belonged to Ted and Susie Field. He's a son of the late Marshall Field, the department-store magnate. *Forbes* magazine estimates his net worth at $500 million. He's thirty-seven years old. Nice work if you can get it.

"What should I wear?" I asked. "Is it dressy? I have a suit, though I don't suppose anyone in California wears suits, do they?"

"You mean, since David Niven died?"

"I want to dress appropriately for the Amazon rain forest. Either I wear a suit—or a flannel shirt and carry a chain saw."

I was told to report to Beverly Hills High School, where guests would board shuttle buses to the Fields' home. The tone of the evening was set when I drove up and found Beverly Hills High had valet parking.

The ride took ten minutes. (I sat next to a couple who'd just bought a Range Rover for their live-in maid. "She likes to ski," they explained.) The grounds were decorated to approximate a rain forest. Great, lush ferns were everywhere, brightly colored in the tropical yellow, orange, red, and blue hues you see on parrots. They even pumped in humidity. Actually, it felt like the Rock Creek tennis courts in late July. You want rain forest? Go north on Sixteenth, turn left.

Celebrity-spotting was a cinch. Mingling among some studio execs and some trophy wives were Tom Selleck,

Don Johnson, Jeff Bridges, Ted Danson, Martin Short, Kevin Costner, Ed Begley, Jr., Norman Lear, Goldie Hawn. Each was taller, shorter, or thinner than I thought—except Ed Begley, Jr., whom I never think about.

There was a tent, and my table was near the back. Any further, it would've been in Nevada, but who's complaining? I'm at a Beverly Hills mansion the size of the Pentagon, I'm eating fancy food, and Bruce Springsteen is about to play. I'm going to bitch about this? (I overheard Martin Short's wife gushing, "I can't believe we got invited! I'm going to hear Springsteen in someone's backyard! I couldn't tell my friends—they'd hate me." Her friends were probably in somebody else's backyard watching Paul McCartney. I couldn't tell *my* friends—they'd tell me to steal the towels.)

Billy Crystal emceed. He did a sports routine beginning with the amazing Tyson-Douglas fight: "At least Buster Douglas acknowledged he was hurt when he went down for ninety-four seconds—he was down longer than Tyson's last fight! Usually boxers don't cop to it. Tyson once hit Trevor Berbick so hard, Trevor did the dance Ann-Margret did in *Bye Bye, Birdie*. Did he hurt you, Trevor? 'I was stunned, that's all, stunned.'" Crystal then recalled a high school basketball game where he guarded "a building in a pair of shorts. He comes down the court laughing at me. 'Where you from, Oz?' He's huge. I can't tell exactly how huge because he's like cloud cover. But his crucifix is so large, it has a real guy on it."

After a film about the destruction of the Amazon rain

forest, Sting got onstage, flanked by Herbie Hancock and Branford Marsalis, and sang a haunting, reedy-voiced *My Funny Valentine*. Then he summoned Bruce Hornsby and The Boss.

"Sting told me this was gonna be kind of like a big cook-out in somebody's backyard," Springsteen said in that pseudo–auto-mechanic way he has. "I say, 'What if it rains?' He says, 'We'll pitch a tent.' I say, 'How'll we raise the money?' He says, 'We'll charge heavy for the meal. It's L.A. Nobody'll mind.'"

Grinning, Springsteen strummed an acoustic guitar and sang "The River" and a rocker titled "You Don't Know What You Got Till It's Gone," which—to Sting's overt skepticism—Springsteen claimed was originally recorded by a Jersey group, Johnny Moore and the Lonely Milkmen. "Really, Bruce, the Lonely Milkmen?" Sting teased, then introduced Don Henley, who sang "The End of the Innocence" to Hornsby's choral piano. I sat wide-eyed, totally starstruck. I'm in backyards all the time, and not once have I run into Johnny Moore.

Joking that "it's always been my ambition to create the best garage band in history," Sting called up Paul Simon, who did "Slip Slidin' Away" with Springsteen, Henley, and Sting *singing backup*! (I assumed it was like the NBA All-Star Game where Larry Bird is happy to pass to Michael Jordan for the sheer thrill of playing with him.) Sting closed the performance by leading the others in "Every Breath You Take."

I stood by my seat watching them leave the stage—this

remarkable array of talent—and tried to convince myself this was all real. I gave backyard parties as a kid. We didn't shuttle the guests up in vans; they drove Chevy Novas and Plymouth Furys with their high school graduation tassels hanging on the rearview mirrors. We didn't charge one thousand dollars a head, and we didn't serve lobster and Oregon chardonnay. We had a keg, a record player, and a stack of forty-fives. After a while the only song that got played was "Tonight, Tonight," and couples drifted out of the range of the floodlights and into each other's dreams. All these years and I finally learned the secret: Get a bigger backyard.

Whoop Dreams

It's never too early to plan your summer vacation, and I've got mine.

I'm going to Michael Jordan's Senior Flight School. It's a three-day basketball camp for people over thirty-five in Las Vegas.

I picked it over a few other intriguing adult camps:

1. Big Boris Yeltsin's White Lightning Siberian Lost Weekend. The brochure promises: "Wodka and Women . . . Go shot for shot with the Bo-Man. Get hammered and sickled on the vast Russian steppes—then tumble down the steppes into a refreshing, naturally heated Chernobyl hot tub!"

2. Jack Kevorkian's Go Gently into That Good Night Getaway. "Relax with Dr. Jack for three cool days and one

long night. Get laid back, then get laid down . . . we can arrange for a convenient checkout time."

3. Marshall Applewhite's See You in September or Thereabouts Interplanetary Holiday Journey. "Find your life shrouded in confusion? Get ready for the New Age with computer training. . . . Come celibate with us! Dance to the hypnotic music of Bo and Peep and Do and Ti, with special guests Hale Bopp and the Comets. One free pair of Nikes for each camper." (Unfortunately, this camp recently "shed its container.")

So I'm going to Michael Jordan's camp. Which actually does exist.

My only problem is it costs $15,000.

"Check only—No credit cards," the brochure says.

My friend Gino says it's worth it. He says that having the opportunity to play basketball with Michael Jordan is "like having a catch with Babe Ruth."

"I doubt it," I said. "I imagine I'd be waiting a long time for the Babe to throw the ball back to me."

Anyway, I'm going to raise the $15,000 even if I have to borrow it from Bob Dole.

And I'm going to fly to Vegas and take part in this camp with seventy-one other campers who have this kind of money: mainly baby-booming geezer orthodontists, plastic surgeons, tax accountants, divorce lawyers, and proctologists between five feet eight and five eleven, most of whom will have back hair and be named Bernie.

I have the camp schedule in front of me. It starts with

one full hour for breakfast, which is good, because for $15,000 I want enough time for a second cup of coffee and a cigar—hey, it's Vegas. Then we go take pictures with Michael, which is real good, because for $15,000 I want some proof that Michael Jordan and I were actually together at the camp.

(I'll get three pictures with Michael. One shot will be taken "at the Welcoming Cocktail Party." One will be "with team and coach." And one will be taken "with camp uniform on." I'm looking forward to the picture at the cocktail party, because I can wear normal clothing. But I am not looking forward to pictures with my "camp uniform" on. At my age I would rather be caught in a Turkish steam bath with Sammy "The Bull" Gravano than be photographed in gym shorts and a T-shirt so I look like that dork Richard Simmons.)

Next on the schedule is a "Lecture by Michael Jordan." I'm hoping he plays against type and shares his thoughts on sane nuclear policy in the postcommunist global village. Exhausted by mental gymnastics, we move to a calisthenics session, in which a bunch of fat middle-aged guys who look alarmingly like Newman on *Seinfeld* shoot some threes, then plop down on the court to talk about what they want for lunch.

There's a free-throw session after that, to determine the camp champion, who, presumably, gets some fabulous prize—like an hour with a Vegas showgirl. Then we spend thirty minutes at basketball practice. But only thirty minutes, because nobody wants to overdo the athletic aspect of camp. After that we eat lunch, because, after all, we haven't eaten in, what, three hours? And for $15,000 it better not be a bologna sandwich and a carton of milk. Then we hear a couple of lectures from famous coaches and NBA referees, assuming you can drag these guys away from the slot machines.

I know you worry that at my age I could drop dead guarding Michael Jordan under a hot Las Vegas sun. Well, don't. Michael doesn't actually play. But a spokesman for Michael says, "He'll be out on the court with the campers." So if I do drop dead guarding one of the Bernies, at least Michael will be nearby. And if I need a doctor, perhaps Dr. Julius Erving will be on call.

And if I live, look at what I'll get: a one-hour "professionally done" camp video and a bag filled with "souvenir items from Michael Jordan's corporate partners." (I can really use a pair of Hanes underpants, and a Filet-O'-Fish sandwich from McDonald's. They can keep that new Michael Jordan cologne that smells like a bug bomb, though.)

But the biggest perk of all is that as a camper I can "bring a guest who will be able to observe camps and attend the Welcoming Cocktail Party and our Closing Ceremony Brunch." This is an almost unparalleled opportunity to show off. It's like being able to bring King Hussein to a bar mitzvah. (As my "guest" I'm thinking of bringing a 1,500-pound sow from a 4-H show, just to shake things up.)

Obviously, the only reason to attend Michael Jordan's basketball camp is to come back with stories to tell about "me and Mike." Those are the magic words. You get to say to anybody and everybody, "So Michael Jordan and I were standing at the foul line, and Mike turns to me and he says . . ."

You get that and three nights in Vegas for $15,000.

A night in the Lincoln Bedroom is $150,000.

I'm going with Mike.

What's the Use
Without Dr. Seuss

All day I pondered
On how I would choose
The words that would soften
The damnable news.
That Seuss, the great marvelous
Doctor of rhyme
Who had cheered and begrinned us
So much of the time
Was gone from our midst,
A terrible crime.
So I gathered the children close to my side
To tell them that sadly
The Doctor had died.
The Seuss who wrote Horton
And Yertle and Grinch
Was no longer among us

What's the Use Without Dr. Seuss

Was gone, was kerplinch.
And Lizzie went into a tizzie, oh my
She started to sniffle, to burble, to cry.
(She's eight, you must realize
Not familiar with dying
Not sufficiently worldwise
So of course she was sighing.)
"My doctor?" she asked.
"My pediatrician?"
"Not yours," I responded.
"The Seuss, the clinician
Of birthdays and hatchings
Of purposeless Thneeds
That prompt greedy people
To chop truffula trees."
"Oh, Seuss!" she acknowledged
A smile on her face
"Well, no one, not no one
Can take Seuss's place."
And Michael inquired
His eyes growing wide
"How old was exactly
This Seuss when he died?"
I believed eighty-seven
A rich and ripe age
And wearing a hat
When he went to his grave.
A hat from the cat
Who was hatted so well

Was catted and hatted
And sang like a bell.
He was aimed at the young ones
For giggles and glads
(And not only them
But their moms and their dads)
And he brought them adventure
Some say mischief, I know
But the smiles, oh the smiles
The wonder, the glow.
Now numbers are not something
Michael can figure.
Once he gets over ten
His arithmetic jiggers.
He thinks fathers are all
Pretty much the same age
Eighty-seven or forty
It's a tough thing to gauge.
"Eighty-seven's not old,
You're older than that.
Will you die, too, Daddy?
Will you die in your hat?"
Not hardly, I told him
And hugged both their necks.
"I can't die this week, guys,
Who'll paint the new deck?"
So I lifted them up
On the living room couch
And took out a Seuss book

2 4 8

What's the Use Without Dr. Seuss

And started to grouch
Of the Grinch and the Lorax
And Horton the nester
Of Bartholomew Cubbins
And Yertle that jester,
Who thought all the turtles
Should give him support
And make him the tallest
Of allest, and snort
That no one was taller
Or higher than he
A lesson hard learned
In hu-mil-i-ty.
And I read them of green eggs
And also of ham
How I just do not like them
You Sam, Sam-I-am.
I read them of snorfling
And Whooing and gloots
And brown bar-ba-loots
In their bar-ba-loot suits
And humming-fish humming
While splashing around
In the rippulous pond
With that wonderful sound.
And when I was finished
I closed up the book
Held it near to my heart
With a faraway look

And said, "Michael and Lizzie,
We've just lost a friend
But though Seuss isn't here
His books won't ever end
Providing there's mommies
And daddies who'll read
To their kids before bedtime
To their kids who'll take heed
To celebrate words
Of this rare, silly goose
This genius, this giant
This great Dr. Seuss."

CAPITAL
COMMENT

Try Federal Reserves with Clinton on DL

Washington was stunned by the news that quarterback and team leader Bill Clinton would be out of action for six to eight weeks because of a torn tendon in his right knee. The hopes of most Americans were resting on the charismatic quarterback, who had just been re-signed to a four-year contract.

"This is a real distraction for the team," said a management source. "Clinton was starting to find his rhythm. We had such high hopes for him."

With Clinton sidelined, Al "The Money Store" Gore is expected to move into the starting quarterback spot. But Gore has been injured himself lately—he's suffering with a tender elbow from what doctors have called "putting the arm on too many people for contributions."

It's unclear if Washington will have to enter the free-agent market in search of an unsigned quarterback. The names most prominently mentioned carry baggage that might disqualify them: Madeleine Albright (identity crisis), Jack Kemp (wrong political party), and Heath Shuler (as welcome here as Dick Morris is at a White House dinner).

Clinton had been expected to lead his team through a particularly difficult patch of their schedule in the upcoming months. Starting with a road trip to meet Boris Yeltsin, leader of a tough Russian squad, Clinton was booked for away games in nineteen countries on five continents in the next five months! "They were gonna work him like a plow mule," said a league source. "The thing about Clinton is, he's better on the road than he is at home—I guess he prefers hotel rooms to his own bed. Some guys are like that."

Clinton is expected to recover fully, although there is some concern for his weight while he is inactive. Clinton is known for his tendency to pork up, and there are already reports that he is spending most of his time sitting in front of the TV, watching the NCAA tournament and eating corn dogs. A team source analogized the predicament of having a sedentary Clinton as "like letting John Williams loose in a buffet line."

Clinton's injury was another blow to the Washington sports scene that has been devastated by a rash of departures in recent years of such prominent players as Warren "The Big Unit" Christopher, George "Parallel Park" Stephanopoulos, and Robert "Muggsy" Reich. This has been a bad year for the Bullets and Capitals. Now, with Clinton out at QB—he's officially listed as "DL month-to-month (knee)"—another Washington team may be doomed to a second-division finish.

"We think we have pretty good depth at other positions. But Clinton was the one player we couldn't afford to lose for an extended period of time," a team spokesman said. "Look what's happened to the Spurs without David Robinson. I just hope we get Clinton back faster than we got back Francis Gary Powers."

Team doctors said that the operation to repair a torn tendon in Clinton's right knee was a complete success, and Clinton has already begun rehabilitation. At his age, and in his circumstance, though, every game he misses is an important one. "He's not gonna play forever; he'll be out of the league in three years," the team spokesman acknowledged.

Sports talk radio in the nation's capital was abuzz with the news Clinton would miss up to two months.

"Now what? Gore's supposed to lead the team?" one indignant caller asked. "What's he gonna do to soften his hands—use Formby's deck stain?"

"I told you we should have kept Dole instead of Clinton," said a man who identified himself as Newt from Capitol Hill. "Dole is real old, but at least you always knew where he was at two in the morning—he was sound asleep."

"This is what happens when you give a guy a four-year, no-cut contract," one caller said, complaining. "Now you watch, he's gonna start getting hurt all the time, like Kelvin Bryant."

Photographs of Clinton being wheeled from the hospital caused a minor stir, as they showed Clinton wearing an Adidas sweat suit and New Balance running shoes. (Pushy agent Bird of Prey bragged, "If Clinton would sign with me, I could get him a cologne deal.")

"We're very proud and honored Mr. Clinton chose the comfort of our clothing," Adidas said in a statement.

Spokesmen for Nike, Reebok, and Fila declined comment—although there was a rumor that to do damage control, Nike chairman Phil Knight had flown to Bethesda Naval Center to affix swooshes on the surgical masks of everyone involved in the Clinton operation.

"Clinton wearing Adidas isn't that big a deal," said one casual-apparel industry insider. "They may corner the 'fat white guy in a sweat suit' market. But Nike still has Tiger Woods."

Diary Straits

Bob Packwood's diary. Josh Steiner's diary. Frank Richardson's diary, in which Kimba Wood, the dignified, erudite federal judge, shows up as some married millionaire's lust bunny.

How many more examples do we have to see before we realize that keeping a diary *is the single dumbest, most self-incriminating act of narcissism since Jerry Lewis's talk show?*

(I myself have just finished going over the diary I have kept faithfully since 1966, and I see now that there are some minor inaccuracies, which I would like to correct, for the record, in case my diary ever gets into the wrong hands and is published: specifically, the part about my being on *Apollo 11* with Neil Armstrong. I also make the following correction: The stuff about me sleeping with Ann-Margret on pages 18, 49, 118, 121, 122, 123, 615,

897–912, well, that wasn't Ann-Margret, it was *[Note to copy desk: Please insert name of some famous dish who is currently dead]*. Oh, and it wasn't a banana, it was a cordless phone.)

I mean, why would you keep a diary?

All a diary can do is get you in trouble. (And if that isn't the case, how come when you buy them in the stores they come with locks and keys?) Nixon got the boot, and all he had were tapes. Can you imagine what would have happened if he had a diary, too? Especially if he used the same literary devices as Packwood—confession, melodrama, and very, very, dreadfully bad writing:

"Dear Diary: Today I started the Watergate cover-up. Whoa, Nelly! I sure am skating on a thin limb here without a paddle! If anyone knew, they'd impeach me for sure! Also, I am fond of big hooters."

Packwood got the double whammy from his diary. Not only did the lecherous sex scenes reveal him to be a toad-sucking fungus, but the rambling banalities about supermarkets and hardware stores revealed him to be the kind of maximum bore known as Human Glade—because he clears out a room. Have you read this swill? Packwood is not exactly Samuel Pepys—he's more like Little Bo Pepys.

Losers keep diaries.

You think Denzel Washington keeps a diary? You think Hammerin' Henry Kissinger keeps a diary? Cool guys don't keep diaries. (Cool guys videotape, right, Bob?)

Keeping a diary is an immature impulse based on the egomaniacal delusion that the world revolves around ME, so everything that happens to ME is important. ME, not you. If you are in MY diary, you just exist as a prop to make ME look good. (I suppose this is the proper spot for me to confess that I recently, ahem, came into possession of my daughter's old diary, and I saw entries that could have embarrassed ME if they became public. Such as: "Everybody thinks my dad is funny because he writes that newspaper column. The truth is that his friends Nancy and Gino actually write it. My dad hasn't written one word of that column in six years. My dad isn't even slightly funny, and after he eats dinner he burps like a tommy gun." So every time I came across a reference critical of ME, I changed it to "Art Buchwald." Pretty slick, huh?)

What I really like about Packwood is his saying now how his diary contains "inaccuracies." This means he wrote stuff down that didn't happen. I know about that because my scorecards in golf often contain "inaccuracies." I make a 7 and I write down 5. I also sometimes enter scores for a nonexistent partner, to make myself look good. Then, years later when I consult my scorecards (I keep them all in my golf bag, sort of like a diary), I say to myself, "Well, lookee here, I shot a seventy-six at Woodmont in August of 1991, including an eagle three on the treacherous five-hundred-eighty-six-yard tenth. I must've been hitting the hell out of it that day. I beat my pal Seve Ballesteros by four strokes!"

To use golf terminology, this is considered "improving one's lie."

Packwood doctored up the sex parts to make himself

look like more of a stud. So in a way he was improving his, er, lie, too.

The lamest excuse that any of these people give for keeping tapes or diaries is that they intend to write their memoirs someday, and they want to be historically accurate. Oh, please. A true history is seldom flattering to the participants. No senator is going to write, ". . . and then President Kennedy asked me a question, which I later found out was about what he should do about the missiles in Cuba, but I missed it because I was preoccupied with digging this big ball of wax, the color of espresso, out of my ear, and I said, 'Huh?' And then the next time the president spoke to me it was to ask me to go around the corner to a deli and get him and Bobby a couple bologna sandwiches and Dr. Brown's Cel-Ray sodas."

Which is why, when I write my memoirs, I am going to reveal that I was Deep Throat.

Discover the World,
Ski D.C.

Oh, hello. I didn't see you come in. I was just resting after a harrowing few hours of celebrating the city and discovering the world. First I drove to Georgetown so I could celebrate overpricing. But my car was towed and I discovered the world of impounding. I ransomed the car and headed toward the monuments, but I missed my turn and got swept along Route 66 halfway to Front Royal. Coming back on the Whitehurst Freeway, I tumbled into a pothole the size of an archaeological dig and had to take a taxi home. My driver got hopelessly lost in Rock Creek Park; his last words before I got out to walk were "Is not so many forest where I am born."

I suppose "Celebrate the City, Discover the World" is a nice enough slogan, though I preferred: "Washington, I Miss You," obviously a submission from Lorton.

I wish I'd known about the contest. I'd have entered slogans more in tune with the current spirit of the city. Put these on the license plates:

Washington: Keep Low.

D.C.: It's Not *That* Bad.

Bitch Set Me Up.

Discover D.C.: Buy a Cabbie a Map.

Washington: All It's Cracked Up to Be.

Holding Cell on the Potomac.

Make Bail.

Land of Sirens.

Live Expensively and Die.

Ski Washington. Snow All Year Round.

Pavement May Crumble, Real Estate May Tumble, but Humidity Is Here to Stay.

911. Please Hold.

Last Stop Before Rehab.

The Nation's Capital: Your Bucks Stop Here.

Gateway to Gaithersburg.

Don't Kill *Me*.

Honk If You've Tooted With the Mayor.

Stan Parris Doesn't Sleep Here.

Explore 10,000 Potholes.

We're Hot. We're Weird. We're Here.

Bureaucrats Do It Eventually.

Jesse. Film at 11.

I Don't Brake for Lawyers.

Keep Your Pipe in Your Eyeglass Case and Your Eyes on the Road.

My Parents Went to D.C. and All They Brought Me Back
Was One Lousy Rock of Crack Cocaine.

911. Still Holding.

We Are Broke. Send Money.

I found it odd that the winner of the slogan contest,
Richard M. McWalters, didn't actually reside in the
District, but in the Virginia 'burbs. Instead of that free
weekend, his prize could have been a house here, so he
could feel the thrill of having his property tax raised 22
percent at the same time that his real estate value is dropping off the cliff.

What's It All a Pout, Newtie?

Dear Cousin Alice,

I'm so sorry you had to cancel your long-awaited trip to Washington because the government shut down. But it *is* silly to come to Washington when the tourist attractions are closed. The only way you could get into Arlington National Cemetery last week was to die.

You are better off not coming right now anyway, as we found out that the drinking water was contaminated. One of the last acts of the federal government was to order the D.C. government to do something about the water.

Unfortunately, the D.C. government was forced to shut down, too. (Not that anyone has noticed any change from when it was open.) The only D.C. workers still on the job are police officers, firefighters, and meter maids. So to cope with the water crisis, D.C. ordered the meter maids to write tickets on anyone who drank the water.

You're probably wondering how the government could actually close. And since I've lived in Washington for a while, you probably expect me to guide you through the political labyrinth, and explain the nuances of a balanced-budget proposal and the deconstruction of the Social Security entitlement.

So bear with me, Alice, because this gets complicated.

The nearest I can figure is that 800,000 federal government workers had to walk out of work because Newt "Hey, I've Got Feelings, Too" Gingrich didn't like his seat on *Air Force One*. He wasn't sitting close enough to Bill Clinton. I guess Newt wanted to ride shotgun and control the radio, like in high school. (Although right there in the official photo released by the White House, there's Newtie on the plane sitting at the same table with Clinton. And the inside of the plane appears rather roomy; it seems to have roughly the dimensions of a polo field. I mean, it looks like you could land *another* plane in there.)

The Newtster got steamed because he got bumped to the back of the plane on the flight to Yitzhak Rabin's funeral. How dare they put the House speaker in the back? He's not some minor Hollywood Square, like Shadoe Stevens. He's not B-list. Everybody knows the back of the plane bites. It takes the stews forever to get you a drink. You get plastic cups, not china. You have to pay for your headset. By the time they get to you, all they have left to eat is chicken burgoo. And the seat doesn't recline. It's like trying to sleep in a VW Beetle.

Not only that, but they made Newt get off through the rear of the plane. You know, like a freaking yabbo.

"This is petty," Gingrich conceded.

Aw, I wouldn't say it's petty, Newtie. Condemning a man to die in the gas chamber because you didn't get honey-roasted peanuts is petty. But putting 800,000 people out of work because you felt you should have had a sleeper seat is completely reasonable. Bill Clinton should have brought you up to first class and talked about the budget with you all the way to Israel and back. I mean, what else could he have had on his mind? Jeez, the inhospitable way Clinton was acting, you'd think he was going to a funeral or something.

People have reacted much more intemperately than you, Newt, for far less reason—that guy from Connecticut, for example, who did caca doody on the plane's food cart because they wouldn't give him another drink. You behaved much better than that, Newt. You didn't even pee in Leon Panetta's iced tea. You're a great American, Newt. And next time, dammit, you're riding up front. The pilot will give you a hat to wear, and a lollipop.

So what we have are the two most powerful men in America today (not counting Michael Eisner), Clinton and Gingrich, sending the government of the United States into exile over an issue of respect. What is this, *The Godfather*? Is Newt going to send Tessio to arrange a meeting with Clinton? Does Donna Shalala sleep with the fishes?

For this we had to close the Grand Canyon?

The confusing thing about the shutdown is that the workers were furloughed to save money. But later on, when they return, they will be paid for the days they missed. So it will cost the same, and nothing will have been produced! This is like trying to save money on a new car by saying you'll take the bus to work for six months—but not actually going to work because you don't like the bus, so you lose your job, forcing you to get work as a janitor in a car dealership, where you get a great deal on a new Camry, so you borrow the money from a guy named Angelo "The Septum" Ignozzi. Uh, I think.

I have to admit I have some fear for the continued good health of the republic when they all go back to work. Eight hundred thousand nonessential government workers, including Al Gore, will have spent so much time watching Rolonda and Ricki. What will they think about America now? How will they content themselves with the prosaic administration of national safety standards when it's so much more exciting to be an Eskimo lesbian whose fantasy is to have sex with the daughter of her dentist's uncle?

What astounds me about this shutdown is that it seems to have been good for the country.

The stock market is way up.

The president's popularity is at a new high. (That, of course, is relative. A few weeks ago, most Americans would have voted for Mussolini ahead of Clinton. This week Clinton pulled even with Ross Perot's barber.)

The Democrats are crowing.

Representative Joe Kennedy said, "It doesn't get much better than this."

The people who were elected to run the government have precipitated a shutdown of that very government. Closed. Padlocked. And now they are gloating, IT DOESN'T GET MUCH BETTER THAN THIS!

Have we gone through the looking glass, Alice?

Acknowledgments

My special thanks to Jeanne McManus and Gene Wein-garten, who came up with the ideas for every one of these columns, then wrote them while I was busy making radio and television appearances. And to my dog, Maggie, for eating the piece of paper with the other acknowledgments on it. Oh, and to Eleanor Roosevelt for being the wind beneath my wings.

P.S. And Jennifer, you know who you are.

ABOUT THE AUTHOR

TONY KORNHEISER is in the Witness Protection Program.